The
ANSWER
is always
"JESUS"

The
ANSWER
is always
"JESUS"

74 CHILDREN'S SERMONS & STORIES

Aram Haroutunian

Healthy Life Press
Orlando, Florida

THE ANSWER IS ALWAYS "JESUS"

Published by:

Healthy Life Press – 2603 Drake Drive – Orlando, FL 32810
www.healthylifepress.com

About the Cover: The cover photo depicts the author
with his favorite Palm Sunday "prop," "Firecracker."

Cover Design: Judy Johnson
Internal Design: Judy Johnson

Printed in the United States of America

Library of Congress Cataloging-in-Publication Data
Haroutunian, Aram
   The Answer is Always "Jesus"

ISBN 978-1-4700-7195-0

1. Children's Sermons; 2. Children's Bible Stories

ACKNOWLEDGEMENTS

I would like to thank the following people (and four-legged friends) for their help with this book:

The many folks at Lookout Mountain Community Church who continually urged me to do this project over the fifteen years I was there. And Peter Hiett, whose creativity and preaching were a model and inspiration for me, and who I coordinated with each weekend to make both "sermons" integrate into a seamless whole in the flow and theme of the weekend.

Scotty Sawyer, who read my earliest manuscript, and subsequent additions along the way, and whose encouragement and input kept me going. And whose endless encouragement keeps me going.

Dave Biebel, who kept pursuing me to do this, and without whom this project could not have happened.

My wife Ellen, whose creativity and thinking and vision for the Church is unlike anyone I've ever known. And our two kids, Lauren and Jared, whose creativity far surpasses my own.

And finally, I'm thankful for all the kids at Lookout Mountain Community Church, most of whom are "grown up" now, who brought these sermons to life, and gave us beautiful, poignant, and hysterically funny moments we'll never forget. And, oh yeah, for "Firecracker" (who is on the cover photo with me) and "Vera" (who absolutely refused to let me ride her, and knocked me onto my behind with a few hundred palm-waving children and parents looking on).

Contents

The chapter list is alphabetized. No other prioritization is implied.

- The Strategy of the Children's Sermon
- The Role of the Children
- The Role of the Adults
- The Creative Process
- Preparation and Coordination
- The Role of Humor
- The Role of Objects and Props
- The Format

Introduction

You may have heard the proverbial story of the pastor who was giving the children's message during church. On a particular Sunday, he was using squirrels for an object lesson on industry and preparation. He started out by saying, *"I'm going to describe something, and I want you to raise your hand when you know what it is."* The children nodded eagerly.

"This thing lives in trees (pause) and eats nuts (pause) . . ." No hands went up. *"And it is gray (pause) and has a long bushy tail (pause) . . . "* The children were looking at each other, but still no hands raised. *"And it jumps from branch to branch (pause) and chatters and flips its tail when it's excited (pause) . . ."*

Finally one little boy tentatively raised his hand. The pastor breathed a sigh of relief and called on him. *"Well,"* said the boy, *"I know the answer must be Jesus . . . but it sure sounds like a squirrel to me!"*

In our church community we often joke that the answer to every children's sermon is Jesus. Yet it is also true for adult sermons. Instead of "three keys to successful living" or "ten principles for a better marriage," our church has strived to live according to a core belief that the purpose of preaching is to simply lift up Jesus – and make Him look good. *"And I, if I am lifted up from the earth, will draw all peoples to Myself"* (John 12:32).

Preaching Jesus moves us toward encountering Him at His communion table, and offers an opportunity to be romanced by Him in our hearts as our minds are stimulated and our souls stirred by His gospel.

The children's sermon can play a vital role in this overarching goal of lifting up Jesus. It is designed to entice both children and adults alike with the wonder and mystery of who Christ is. I've found that a good barometer of whether or not a children's sermon is New Covenant-oriented is to observe where it ends. Children's sermons that are Old Covenant-oriented usually end with *the focus on themselves and what they need to do* to earn God's favor. New Covenant-oriented children's sermons usually end by showing *how incredible Jesus is* – which is the starting point for our transformation.

I believe there are simply no hard-and-fast formulas that guarantee "successful living." And just what is "successful living"? As the apostle

Paul declared, *"We preach Christ crucified, to the Jews a stumbling block and to the Greeks foolishness, but to those who are called, both Jews and Greeks, Christ the power of God and the wisdom of God. Because the foolishness of God is wiser than men, and the weakness of God is stronger than men"* (1 Corinthians 1:23-25). But doesn't everyone preach that? Doesn't every church do that? Preaching Christ crucified is harder than we think.

We need look no further than our children's Bibles to see this. In virtually any edition, you'll be hard-pressed to find pictorial illustrations of Christ's agony in Gethsemane, or of His forsakenness on the Cross. Yet, if we truly believe the Bible, it is precisely within these passages – scenes of sheer trust and courageous sacrifice – where abundant life and true joy are to be found. ("Looking unto Jesus . . . who for the joy that was set before Him endured the cross, despising the shame . . ." Hebrews 12:2).

I see a parallel in what has happened to the old children's fables in recent years. It is intriguing to see how many of those old, difficult stories have been either eliminated from our children's libraries or revised for the *modern* young reader. Our reasoning is simple: "How could we ever allow our children to read something so shocking, so bewildering, so violent?" We convince ourselves that we're protecting our children from the harsh realities of the world by excising those difficult passages. Yet we're left wondering why our children struggle when their fragile faith bumps up against the same harsh realities they encounter in the world.

The truth is, we live in a wild and unpredictable world. But we have been given such great hope! The good news is that there is a passionate, wild God-Man who rules over it all and who loves us. And He promises to always be in us – no matter what our circumstances – assuring us that "He who is in you is greater than he who is in the world" (1 John 4:4).

Principles and strategies entice the mind, and even appeal subtly to our flesh's desire for knowledge and control (which is to eat from the tree of the knowledge of good and evil). But Jesus is the only one who can captivate both our minds and hearts. He gives us something (or Someone) that is beyond ourselves to live for – something adventurous, grand, and wild. Yet Jesus is not for the tame of heart. A stroll though the four gospels makes this evident. So, why do we insist on taming our children's hearts – giving them prescriptions to order and control their lives – when we know better? A New Covenant approach to life will be *descriptive* of Jesus rather than *prescriptive*. It is to embrace the incredible mystery and paradox of the Gospel (*"For whoever desires to save his life will lose it; but whoever loses his life for My sake will save it"* Luke 9:24). Ironically, children are more able to grasp these concepts than are we adults. And yet, I have observed that of all places where the spirit of the New Covenant is violated most frequently, it is in children's curricula and children's sermons. *"Do good things to others, and good things will happen to you." "Live in a godly way, and things will turn out great for you."* We set our children up for disappointment by instilling in them (albeit unintentionally) a belief in a "push-button God." And we're as surprised as they are when their alleged faith crashes upon the rocks of harsh reality once they leave home.

We think we need to explain to them every mystery and paradox of God – that this will adequately equip their minds. But all the while – just like us – they're longing to be captivated in their hearts by something bigger. They want to encounter Someone who can't be reduced to a set of principles, Someone who promises to fulfill their young hearts' desire for adventure and wonder.

In our quest to present to them a well-ordered, logical, manageable God (one that we adults often want), our children have been malnourished on a junk-food diet of easy explanations and faulty formulas. Meanwhile, their hearts and souls and minds are starving for what they truly long for – and need – to pursue life in such a baffling, perplexing world. I've become convinced that the question we need to be concerned with, as Elie Wiesel brilliantly observed, is not "Why God?" or "Where is God?" but rather, "*Who* is this God?"

Herein lies the role of the children's sermon. Its purpose, above all other objectives, is to *entice and captivate the heart*, both in children and in adults. This is accomplished by sermons that both *appeal to the mind* (via creativity) and *stir the soul*. How do we do this? Simply by lifting up Jesus.

I'd also like to say a few words about the intended audience of this book: parents and pastors. Most parents nowadays struggle with how to instill the teachings of Jesus into the lives of their children. As I talk with parents, there are very few who practice "family devotions" for many and various reasons. Many feel overwhelmed, ill equipped, or intimidated by the thought. My hope is that the pages ahead might inspire parents toward the simple art of *interactive storytelling* – which captivates the hearts of children. Note: while these children's sermons were developed and delivered in a church context, and were written initially with the pastor in mind, most are easily adaptable for home, campfire, and other family settings.

As for pastors, many preaching pastors I talk with are (surprisingly) terrified at the thought of doing children's sermons. Some are terrified at the prospect of the children's unpredictable responses (which I find to be the *best* part of doing children's sermons!) and want no part of it, or they feel inadequate to do it and need help. Recently, a pastor friend – who had just started a position in a new church – contacted me when she discovered that she would need to do a children's sermon in addition to the adult sermon. She said, "Aram help! I need you to help me with this!" Now this was a person who is one of the finest teachers and preachers I know, and who has taught her entire life – including youth. This book will hopefully help with such feelings, as it provides a window into the thought process in developing and delivering children's sermons, and how to "go with the flow" as you learn to welcome and interact with the children and their wonderful, enthusiastic responses. For pastors and teachers who plan on using children's sermons in a corporate/church setting, I have included an Appendix which provides helpful specifics concerning the development, process, and coordination of the children's sermon in this context.

Advent Wreath – Week 1
The Prophecy Candle

Scripture

2 Peter 1:19

"And so we have the prophetic word confirmed, which you do well to heed as a light that shines in a dark place, until the day dawns, and the morning star rises in your hearts."

Big Idea

As we wait for the coming of Christ in our lives, we need prophetic words from God – which bring encouragement and hope.

Materials

Advent wreath – purple candle (royal color), matches, extra candle to light the advent candle(s) with.

Overview

Advent marks the beginning of the Christian year. It is a season of waiting – waiting for the coming Jesus into our lives. Advent literally means "coming." It is a time of preparation – and it roughly parallels the time of Lent, which leads to Easter. Advent is a time when we ask, *"How and where is God calling me to wait in my life right now? And what is being revealed to me about the nature of God in the midst of my waiting?"* As Job waited on God for answers to his suffering, God never directly answered his questions; but what God did was to reveal more of God to Job. Often times God's self- revelation is in direct antithesis to a lie I may have been believing about Him, or myself. The season of Advent is kind of like a pregnancy. During Advent we ask, *"What is God birthing (or desiring to birth) in me right now?"*

The Advent wreath had its beginnings with the Scandinavian peoples. When winter would set in, the story goes that they would remove one wheel from their wagon – slowing down their activity and forcing them to learn to wait. Imagine if we all did that with our cars: if we removed one wheel and then brought it inside and decorated it, and kept it in our house during the season of Advent? That would sure slow us down!

Sermon

Does anybody know what season this is? [Kids usually will say, "Fall" or "Winter" or "Christmas."] *This is the time of year we call "Advent." Advent means "coming" – and it refers to the coming of who?* [Jesus.] *To celebrate Advent, we use the Advent wreath. The Advent wreath had its beginnings with the Scandinavian peoples. When winter would set in, the story goes that they would remove one wheel from their wagon – slowing down their activity and forcing them to learn to wait. Imagine if we all did that with our cars: if we removed one wheel and then brought it inside and decorated it, and kept it in our house during the season of Advent? That would sure slow us down, wouldn't it? The first candle we're going to light is called the "prophecy" candle. Does anyone know what "prophecy" means? Prophecy can be thought of as "a word from God that brings encouragement and hope." When all is dark, or when you're hoping for God to bring light into some area of your life, a prophetic word from God can bring great encouragement and hope.* [Light the purple candle.] *Let me now read a verse from the Bible which talks about our need for prophetic words from God – it's 2 Peter 1:19 ("And so we have the prophetic word confirmed, which you do well to heed as a light that shines in a dark place, until the day dawns, and the morning star rises in your hearts.") Who do you think this "morning star" is? It's Jesus!* [Note: some good songs which correspond to this week's focus include "O Come O Come Emmanuel" and "Come Thou Long Expected Jesus."]

Prayer

Lord, thank You for this season of Advent; teach us to wait on You and for the new and unique ways You want to come to us and reveal Yourself to us this season. Amen.

Advent Wreath – Week 2
The Bethlehem Candle

Scriptures

Matthew 2:6
"But you, Bethlehem, in the land of Judah, are not the least among the rulers of Judah; for out of you shall come a Ruler who will shepherd My people Israel."

Luke 2:12
"And this will be the sign to you: You will find a Babe wrapped in swaddling clothes, lying in a manger."

Big Idea

This candle reminds us that God "became small" – and enters into the messy places of our lives.

Materials

Advent wreath – red candle (red reminds you of the clay of the earth), matches, candle to light with.

Overview

The mystery and the wonder of the incarnation is that God came to us – becoming one of us – being born in us as we receive Him by faith. The Bethlehem candle reminds us how God "became small" – and not only that, His birth in a stinky, messy stable reminds us how He does not "shirk back" from the messiness of humanity – and of our very lives. This candle prompts the question, "What "messes" in my life have I not believed or allowed God to touch with His presence? How has pride prevented me from receiving God's grace?

Sermon

Now who remembers what season this is? What did we say last weekend? Remember how we celebrate this season with the Advent wreath. Do you remember what "Advent" means? ["Coming."] What do we primarily "do" during the season of Advent? [Wait.] Last weekend we lit the first candle of Advent. Do you remember which candle that was? [The "Prophecy" candle.] *What did we say about "prophecy" – what does it mean?* [It's a word from God that brings encouragement and hope. Re-light the prophecy candle.] *This week we light the second candle of Advent. Now let me ask you a question. If a great and powerful king were to be born in the world, where do you think he would be born?* [One child responded, "In a hospital!" But others responded, "In a palace!"] *Yes – you'd think that a king would be born in a palace – probably in a big, important capital city. But let me ask you: Where was Jesus born?* [One child responded, "In Bethle-home!"] *Was Bethlehem a big city? Actually, it was a small town just outside of Jerusalem. And not only this, but remember – exactly where in Bethlehem was Jesus born?* [In a stable – and then laid in a manger.] *Do you know what a "manger" is? It's an animal feeding trough! Now think about that: Have you ever seen animals eat? It's disgusting! There's spit and drool and chewed up food and slobber all over the place! Jesus was laid in that kind of mess! What does that tell me about Jesus? That He's not afraid of being in messy places – kind of like . . . us.* [Now light the Bethlehem candle.] *If God were born in a palace in some great city, we might be afraid or intimidated by Him – and not feel like He could ever love or care about us. But He comes to small and messy places – like our hearts. Isn't that cool? Let's pray . . .*

Prayer

Jesus, thank You for becoming small and for being born into the messy places in our lives. Thank You that our messiness doesn't disgust You or scare You off. Thank You for loving us when we were still sinners. In Your name, Amen.

Advent Wreath – Week 3
The Shepherds' Candle

Scriptures

Luke 2:15-18

"So it was, when the angels had gone away from them into heaven, that the shepherds said to one another, 'Let us now go to Bethlehem and see this thing that has come to pass, which the Lord has made known to us.' And they came with haste and found Mary and Joseph, and the Babe lying in a manger. Now when they had seen Him, they made widely known the saying which was told them concerning this Child. And all those who heard it marveled at those things which were told them by the shepherds."

2 Timothy 4:5

"But you be watchful in all things, endure afflictions, do the work of an evangelist, fulfill your ministry."

Big Idea

The shepherds came to Jesus; and upon being with Jesus, they then went out and simply told others what they heard and saw.

Materials

Advent wreath – green candle (green reminds you of the fields), matches, candle to light with.

Overview

The shepherds were ordinary, common folk who tended their sheep in the fields. When the angels appeared to them and announced the birth of Jesus, the Scripture says that they did two things: They *came to Jesus*; and then they *went out* and simply told others all that they had seen and heard. And when people heard their report, they "marveled." The shepherds were the first evangelists. So often we feel uncomfortable when we hear the word "evangelism" – either paralyzed with fear; or frustrated by feelings of guilt and manipulation – feeling it to be an unwanted "duty" rather than a labor of love. The story of the shepherds is instructive to us: it is in *coming to Jesus* – and being *with Him* – that one's heart will be reborn and will overflow with a desire to share this birth with others.

Sermon

Now who remembers what season this is? Remember how we celebrate this season with the Advent wreath? Do you remember what "Advent" means? ["Coming."] *What do we primarily "do" during the season of Advent?* [Wait.] *Two weekends ago we lit the first candle of Advent. Do you remember which candle that was?* [The "Prophecy" candle.] *What did we say about "prophecy" – what does it mean?* [It's a word from God that brings encouragement and hope. Re-light the prophecy candle.] *And what was the candle we lit last week?* [The Bethlehem Candle.] *What's so significant about Bethlehem?* [That's just it – there's not much significant about it!] *It's a small town – and remember how we said that this is encouraging – because God became small for us! And we also talked about where within Bethlehem where exactly was Jesus born?* [In a stable, and then laid in a food trough!] *And food troughs are disgusting and messy – which is really cool, because this tells us that God is not afraid to be born in messy places – like us!* [Re-light the Bethlehem candle.] *Now we come to the third candle – which is pink in color. This is the "Shepherd's candle."* [Light it.] *What's so important about the shepherds? What did they do in the Christmas story?* [Several of the kids said, "They brought him gifts!" – confusing the shepherds with the wise men from the East.] *Well, the Bible says (in Luke) that the shepherds came and saw Jesus. And after they saw Him, what did they do? Did they fall asleep?* [No!] *Well, what did they do? They went out and told everybody what they saw and all they heard about Jesus! It's that simple. They were the first "evangelists." Do you know what an "evangelist" is? Simple: someone who simply tells others the good news. They're like people who deliver the newspaper . . . one on every doorstep, announcing to everyone the good news. What's the good news?* [That Jesus was born to die for our sins.] *Let's pray . . .*

Prayer

Lord, thank you for entrusting the message of the good news to common, ordinary people like shepherds – and like us. Lord help us to always come to You and see You in all we do so that we might then tell others about You, Jesus, and all You have done in us. Amen.

Advent Wreath – Week 4
The Angels' Candle

Scripture

Luke 2: 13-14
"And suddenly there was with the angel a multitude of the heavenly host praising God and saying: 'Glory to God in the highest, and on earth peace, goodwill toward men!'"

Big Idea

Angels interrupt our "regularly scheduled programming" to bring us important announcements which change our lives.

Materials

Advent wreath – purple candle (royal color), matches, extra candle to light the advent candle(s) with.

Overview

Angels are intimidating creatures. Most of the time, when you see them show up in Scripture, their first words are, "Fear not!" Angels have a way of disrupting things – of interrupting the normal course of events for special announcements from heaven. When they show up, you know something's up . . . something's terribly important that demands your full attention. Their announcements remind me of when special bulletins or special reports interrupt "regularly scheduled programming" on TV: "We interrupt this regularly scheduled programming to bring you the following important announcement!" Such announcements are rare; but when they come, you know that, chances are, your life will never be the same. Such an announcement was heralded by the angels that day.

Sermon

[Review each of the past three weeks; light each of the three preceding candles as you do.] *Now we come to the fourth week of Advent – Who came from the sky in the Christmas story?* [Several yelled out, "Jesus!" – to which I responded, "No – you're jumping ahead on me!] *What scary-looking beings appeared to the shepherds in the sky?* [Angels!] *What do angels "do"?* [At this point, one child blurted out, "They fly!"] *Yes, they fly! But what else do they do? Does anyone know?* [They bring messages from God. Light the 4th candle.]

Let me ask you: how many of you watch TV? Have you ever had this happen – when you're watching TV, and all of the sudden the screen goes blank and you hear this (say this with a deep, television-like voice): "We interrupt this regularly scheduled programming to bring you the following important announcement." What happens when you hear that? Doesn't your heart start beating? Aren't you anxious about what the announcement's going to be? Often times such announcements are very important messages – announcements that can change your life. They "interrupt" the "regularly scheduled programming" and change everything! That's what happened with the angels' announcement: Jesus is born – and life on the earth would never again be the same!

Prayer

Lord, thank You for coming to our world with messages of good tidings for all the people. Thank You for changing our world forever. Thank You for coming into our lives – so that our lives will never be the same. Help us not to be afraid of Your coming to us – but to trust You and follow You wherever You lead us. Amen.

Advent Wreath – Week 5
The Christmas Candle

Scriptures

Isaiah 9:2
"The people who walked in darkness have seen a great light; those who dwelt in the land of the shadow of death, upon them a light has shined"

John 1:4-5
"In Him was life, and the life was the light of men. And the light shines in the darkness, and the darkness did not comprehend it"

John 8:12
"Then Jesus spoke to them again, saying, 'I am the light of the world. He who follows Me shall not walk in darkness, but have the light of life.'"

John 8:12
"And have no fellowship with the unfruitful works of darkness, but rather expose them. For it is shameful even to speak of those things which are done by them in secret. But all things that are exposed are made manifest by the light, for whatever makes manifest is light. Therefore He says: 'Awake, you who sleep, Arise from the dead, And Christ will give you light.'"

Materials

Advent wreath, white candle, matches, extra candle to light the advent candle(s) with.

Big Idea

Jesus is the light in a world filled with darkness.

Overview

In our church we have a tradition of celebrating Christmas on Christmas Eve with candlelight services. There is a tremendous sense of anticipation, for this is what we've been leading up to the past month in celebrating Advent with the Advent candles. Now, the time of waiting is about to end: Christ is born in our dark world; and His light shines in the dark places – not only in the world, but the dark places of our lives – where we tend to feel despair, abandonment, or hopelessness. Jesus has not forsaken us! He has come to us, and shines His light on the dark places. And "all things that are exposed are made manifest by the light, for whatever makes manifest is light." This is the good news! All we need to do is confess – and Jesus will transform any areas of darkness in our hearts – and in our lives – into pure light.

Sermon

OK – we're finally here! We've been waiting patiently during the past four weeks during the season of Advent. Do you all remember each candle that we lit? Let's go back and review. [Review each candle, and light each one as you do.] Now we come to the last candle – which is in the middle. Which candle is this? Yes! The Christ candle! Jesus is born in our world – and He is the light of the world! What happens when light shines in darkness? [It becomes light.] Isn't that amazing? And isn't that comforting? Darkness doesn't stand a chance! If it's exposed to the light, it can't be darkness any more – but it becomes light – and all shadows disappear! That's how it is with us: if there are any areas of our lives where we're feeling guilt, or shame, or despair, or fear; what Jesus wants us to do is to simply confess it to Him – and He'll shine His light on it – and it will no longer have any power over us – because it will now become light! Praise God! The light of the world has come!

Prayer

Jesus, thank You that You are the light of the world. Please shine Your light on all the dark places of my life – places that I'm afraid to reveal to You and others because I'm afraid of what You or others will think. Thank You that I don't need to be afraid – because Your light is pure love – and it transforms all that is dark into light and love! Thank You for coming into the world. Happy Birthday, Jesus!

All Saints' Day 1

(do this the week leading up to Halloween)

Scripture

Hebrews 12:1
"Therefore we also, since we are surrounded by so great a cloud of witnesses . . . let us run with endurance the race that is set before us"

Ephesians 3:14-15
"For this reason I bow my knees to the Father of our Lord Jesus Christ, from whom the whole family in heaven and earth is named . . . ."

Big Idea

All Saints' Day is a day to celebrate resurrection life; and to remember those Christians who have gone before us, who (specifically) helped us to get to know Jesus.

Materials

Pastoral (formal) robe; white lily.

Overview

Halloween (and the question of how to observe it, or whether to observe it at all) is a very controversial subject in the Church. Rather than taking a negative approach, or ignoring it altogether, I decided to tackle it head-on: through a better alternative, which likely was around long before "All Hallows Eve" ever became popular.

Sermon

[Wearing a robe, use an English "high brow" kind of accent.] *"What holiday is coming up this week? (Halloween!) Halloween shmalloween! Yes, I guess that's coming up . . . but there's another holiday that comes right after Halloween that's even more exciting – a holiday that not too many people know about. Does anyone know what that might be?*

It's "All Saints' Day!" Do you know what a "saint" is? [Quickly tear off the robe and proclaim, now in a Brooklyn kind of voice, *"You're look'n at one!"*] *Actually, everyone who believes in Jesus is a saint . . . but a lot of people have the impression that you have to be perfect to be a saint. But I'm a saint, and I'm not perfect. (Right? ☺) And on "All Saints' Day" we remember all the saints who have gone before us – especially those who helped us get to know Jesus. Now I imagine that for most of you, that might be your parents, or perhaps a grandparent, or a Sunday School teacher . . .*

But for me [tell your own story here] *it wasn't really my parents, but my next door neighbor, Mrs. Back. You see when I was your age, Mrs. Back prayed for me every day. In fact, she prayed for me every day for FIFTEEN YEARS that I would become a Christian! Isn't that amazing? Now I would love to write her a letter to remember her and thank her, but I can't. Do you know why? SHE'S DEAD! But let me ask you: is she really dead? No – she's with the Lord (like the apostle Paul said, "absent from the body, present with the Lord) . . . with all the saints who are there, too! Isn't that exciting? All I'm saying is,* [at this point get the Easter lily and hold it up], *this week, instead of celebrating death, that maybe we should be celebrating life! Let's pray . . .*

Prayer

Lord, thank You for all the saints who have gone before us – those who have prayed for us, loved us, and laid a foundation for us. Help us never forget those who have gone before us, and help us to find encouragement through their stories. Amen.

All Saints' Day 2

Scripture

Ephesians 3:17-19a
"...that Christ may dwell in your hearts through faith; that you, being rooted and grounded in love, may be able to comprehend with all the saints what is the width and length and depth and height, and to know the love of Christ . . ."

Revelation 8:3-4
"Then another angel, having a golden censer, came and stood at the altar. He was given much incense that he should offer it with the prayers of all the saints upon the golden altar which was before the throne. And the smoke of the incense, with the prayers of the saints, ascended before God from the angel's hand"

Hebrews 12:1
"Therefore we also, since we are surrounded by so great a cloud of witnesses, let us run with endurance the race that is set before us . . . ."

Big Idea

God has given us fellow saints to encourage us along our journey of faith.

Materials

Large (picture) book of famous Saints (I used *One Hundred Saints* published by Bulfinch Press, 1993); photo directory of the church.

Overview

Year after year I do this (or a similar version of this) children's sermon on *All Saints' Day*, and each year I'm struck by the fact that very few adults, never mind children, are aware or conscious of this wonderful holiday. All Saints' Day reminds us that we are not alone on the journey. We have a "great cloud of witnesses" – both those who have gone before us, and those who are currently with us – to provide perseverance, encouragement, and a sense of perspective.

Sermon

We have a big holiday coming up this week! Do you know what it is? [Most kids will say "Halloween."] No – it's not Halloween. It's "All Saints' Day." Now let me ask you this: "What's a saint?" I was wondering this myself, so I went looking through my library, and I found this cool book on saints. [Open the book and glance through it.] Wow – look at all these saints! There's St. Augustine, and St. Teresa, and St. Matthew, St. Francis, St. Bernard, St. Ambrose, St. John, St. Veronica, etc. . . . Now, there's a problem with this – you see, all these saints have one thing in common. Do you know what that is? They're ALL DEAD! ☺ So where could we find some saints who are living? I'll show you where – right here! [Take out photo directory of the church.] Look at this! There's Saint Aram and St. Ruth and St. Billy and St. Mike and St. Sherri and St. Katharine . . . ! Isn't that cool? They're all saints! And we're all saints – all of us who belong to Jesus. And God has given us a community of saints because He knows that we can't live this life alone – or we'll get discouraged and lonely. But He gives us a community of saints so that we might love one another and encourage one another – so that we might have hope. Let's pray . . .

Prayer

Lord, thank You for all the saints who have gone before us, and those who are with us. Thank You for their prayers, their love, and their encouragement that has helped us on the journey. Thank You for making me a saint – a "work of art" in progress. Amen.

Arms of Love

Deuteronomy 33:27-28a
"The eternal God is your refuge, and underneath are the everlasting arms; He will thrust out the enemy from before you, and will say, 'Destroy!' Then Israel shall dwell in safety . . ."

Isaiah 53:1
"Who has believed our report? And to whom has the arm of the Lord been revealed?"

1 John 3:1
"Behold what manner of love the Father has bestowed on us, that we should be called children of God!"

Big Idea

As we wait for the coming of Christ in our lives, we need prophetic words from God – which bring encouragement and hope.

Materials

None needed. You will need a small child to volunteer to help you.

Overview

My friend Duncan was the inspiration for this children's sermon. At our weekly staff meeting, Duncan was sharing how his children hate to see him go in the morning, and cling to him at the door as he departs for the office. The night before, his youngest son lunged into his arms, and then with great effort and straining with all his might, tried to wrap his tiny arms around his big father – but to no avail. Duncan shared how, in that moment, it hit him: "It's not important that my son is able to wrap his small arms around me; what's important is that I can wrap my arms around him." And so it is with us, children of God. *"Cease striving, and know that I am God"* (Psalm 46:10)

Sermon

[Scope out the children before you begin – you'll need to find some small children who won't be able to wrap their arms completely around you.] *"How old are you guys?" (Listen to their answers.)"Four? "Six?" "Five?" Wow – you guys are getting really big! But you know what? I bet that none of you can wrap your arms all the way around me! Want to try?"* Pick up several children – have them try to wrap their arms around you. Challenge them and encourage them to try really hard – to stretch with all their might to get their arms around you. *"None of you could get your arms around me! But you know what? I can get my arms around each of you – can't I? Because I'm bigger than you!"* At this point, bend down and wrap your arms around some of kids.*"You couldn't get your arms around me, but I could get my arms around you – because I'm bigger than you! Who does that remind you of?"* [Jesus! Right! The answer to every children's sermon! ☺] *"How does that make you feel? Doesn't that make you feel good? God loves to wrap His big, loving arms around us. He's our "Abba" Daddy – and if we believe in Him, the Bible says we're His children – and if we're His children, He must love to hold us in His arms – and that's the safest place we can ever be."*

Prayer

Lord, forgive us for grasping and striving to control You and for trying to get our arms around You – and for trying to be bigger than You. Help us to submit to You and allow You to hold us in Your outstretched arms – arms that have been pierced . . . for us. Help us to trust You, Lord – and help us to rest in Your arms. In Your name, Amen.

Ash Wednesday

Scripture

Genesis 2:7
"And the Lord God formed man of the dust of the ground; and breathed into his nostrils the breath of life; and man became a living being."

Ezekiel 37:3-6
And He said to me, 'Son of man, can these bones live?' So I answered, 'O Lord God, You know.' Again He said to me, 'Prophesy to these bones, and say to them, "O dry bones, hear the word of the Lord! Thus says the Lord God to these bones: 'Surely I will cause breath to enter into you, and you shall live. I will put sinews on you and bring flesh upon you, cover you with skin and put breath in you; and you shall live. Then you shall know that I am the Lord.'"

John 20:21-22
"So Jesus said to them again, 'Peace to you! As the Father has sent Me, I also send you.' An when He had said this, He breathed on them, and said to them, 'Receive the Holy Spirit.'"

Big Idea

God loves to breathe His Spirit into dry and dead things and bring them to life.

Materials

Small bag or container of ashes (many church supply stores carry ashes that have been made from palm leaves).

Overview

I have found that many churches (outside of Catholic or mainline Protestant denominations) do not celebrate holidays like Ash Wednesday, which I find unfortunate. Holidays like this are beautiful and give opportunity for sacramental expression of the Gospel. That which is sacramental is something which makes invisible realities visible. Ash Wednesday marks the beginning of Lent. Of course it follows "Fat Tuesday" (or "Mardi Gras"). Most of us associate Fat Tuesday with New Orleans and all kinds of debauchery. But in the church calendar, the purpose of Fat Tuesday is to give expression and confession to our "dark side," if you will, the flesh that is at war within us (cf. Paul's descriptive portrayal of this in Romans 7). Having our lusts and our addictions and our flesh thus exposed during this day of "feasting," it ushers us into the season of Lent, which is a time of fasting and denial of this flesh – and drawing closer to Jesus, as we follow Him to the cross – the ultimate expression of self-denial and love for others. Ash Wednesday reminds us of our weakness and limitations, and how our life depends on the very breath of God – which brings life out of death.

Sermon

[Show the kids the dark, black ashes.] *Does anyone know what these are?* [Ashes.] *Do you know what special day it is this coming week? I'll give you a hint: it's on Wednesday.* [Ash Wednesday!] *On Ash Wednesday we take ashes, like these, and we put them on our forehead. Does anyone know why we do this? It reminds us how frail we are – how God made Adam from the dust of the ground, and when we die, our bodies will return to the dust of the ground. But is this the end of us?* [Thank God, NO!!!] *Because God's very breath is in us, and the Bible says that God's life is forever, and His breath won't return to Him void. And God loves taking dead and dry things, like the dust or like old bones, and He loves to breathe His breath into dead and dry things – like us – and bring new life to us. That's the good news of the Gospel! So on Wednesday, when you receive the ashes, the person who puts the ashes on you will say, "You are dust, and to dust you shall return." (That's kind of the bad news.) But then he or she will say, "Repent, and believe the Good News!" Because Jesus loves breathing His very breath into old and dead things, and bringing them to life. That's our hope!*

Prayer

Lord Jesus, thank You that You love to breathe Your breath into us, and to bring dead things to life. Help us surrender the dead things in our life to You, so that You might give us new life! Amen.

Bad News, Good News

Ecclesiastes 5:2
"Do not be rash with your mouth, and let not your heart utter anything hastily before God. For God is in heaven, and you are on earth."

Colossians 1:3, 5-6a
"We give thanks to the God and Father of our Lord Jesus Christ, praying always for you . . . because of the hope which is laid up for you in heaven, of which you heard before in the word of the truth of the good news, which has come to you . . . ."

Big Idea

The Bible reorients us to what is truly real, in the midst of a world that seems to indicate that God is not good, nor in control.

Materials

Newspaper (Front page section – preferably with bad headlines), Bible.

Overview

So often, life seems so random. It takes great faith to believe that there is a God who is totally aware of everything that is going on (especially when He allows things that are so hurtful and devastating). The Bible was given to reorient us to what is truly most real, when everything around us seems most real and heaven seems like a wishful dream.

Sermon

Begin by flipping through the first few pages of today's newspaper, sighing and moaning and shaking your head as you do. Then, begin putting words to your discouragement: e.g. *"Man – look at this: Earthquakes going on in _____, people being killed in the war in _____, fighting in _____, etc. . . ."*

There is so much bad news going on in the world . . . does that ever discourage you? (Yes! I know it sure can discourage me at times.) *Do you ever think that evil is going to win? That God will be defeated? How do we know that God is in control – even though we see so much bad news? Where on earth can I find some good news?* (If they don't say anything, pick up a Bible and start looking at it.) *That's right – in the Bible! And what is the good news found in the Bible? That God is very aware of what is going on in the world – in fact He is so concerned about it that He did something about it! Do you know what He did? He sent His Son, Jesus, into this world to die for our sins – all the fighting, all the hatred – so that we could be forgiven! And so that He could be with us! God knows about everything that is going on in the world – He is not unaware. Isn't that great news? You may never read about it in the newspaper, but it's the best news you could ever hear!*

Prayer

Lord, thank You that You haven't forgotten us. Even though life sometimes seems like things happen randomly and by accident, we know by faith that You are aware of everything and You have good news for us. Help us to trust You Lord, especially when everything around us seems to be falling apart. In Your name, Amen.

Broken Vessels

Scripture

John 7:37-38
"If anyone thirsts, let him come to Me and drink. He who believes in Me, as the Scripture has said, out of his heart will flow rivers of living water. But this He spoke of His Spirit"

Ephesians 5:18
"And do not be drunk with wine, which is dissipation; but be filled with the Spirit."

Psalm 23:5
"You anoint my head with oil; my cup runs over."

Matthew 5:6
"Blessed are those who hunger and thirst for righteousness, for they shall be filled."

Big Idea

The only way you can keep a broken vessel full is to keep it under the faucet. (D.L. Moody)

Materials

Styrofoam (or paper) cup, glass pitcher of water.

Overview

This children's sermon was inspired by the famous quote by D.L. Moody. We are to be like leaky faucets – giving ourselves away as the Lord fills us. If we're filled and we don't give ourselves away, we will become bloated and die. But if we continually give ourselves away and are not filled with Him, we will have nothing to give. It's fascinating to look at what Jesus says in John 7:37-38. He says, "He who believes in Me, as the Scripture has said, *out of his heart will flow* rivers of living water." The flow is *outward*. We simply need to trust that He will continually fill us if we step out in faith and give ourselves away.

Sermon

[Come out with a Styrofoam cup and a glass pitcher of water. The Styrofoam cup should have a small hole in it on the side near the bottom]. *I'm really thirsty this morning . . . mind if I get a drink?* [Pour water into the cup; continue talking to the kids after you fill the cup. At this point, the kids will start screaming, as water will leak out through the hole in the cup onto the floor around them (and even on them!) I acted oblivious to the hole and the leak, and instead acted confused as to why the cup was no longer filled.] *Hey, that's weird . . . I just poured water into my cup and now it's gone . . . I better pour more water into the cup.* [Kids will start screaming again.] *Wow! This cup keeps emptying! What's the problem!* [The kids yelled out, "It's got a hole in it!"] *Oh! The cup has got a leak! It's broken! What should we do?* [One child yelled out, "Get a new cup!"] *Yes – but what if you can't get a new cup? What can I do if I want to get a cup of water?* [Another child yelled out, "Fix the cup!"] *Yes – but what if I can't really fix the cup right now . . . how can I keep this broken cup full? I need to keep filling it with water! I think we're a lot like this broken cup. And the Lord promises to fill us, so that we might continually pour ourselves out for the sake of others, so they might drink. But we need to trust Him! I think sometimes we don't believe He'll be there and He'll fill us, so we hold onto our water or our "stuff" and we don't give ourselves away, and so we hoard things and hold onto them. But God promises that He'll fill us as we give ourselves away for the sake of others.*

Prayer

Lord, help us to believe You and trust that You will indeed fill us up when we give ourselves away for the sake of others and the sake of Your Kingdom. Please help us to trust You, Jesus. Amen.

Chocolate Milk Gospel

Scripture

Ephesians 5:18
"And do not be not drunk with wine, for that is dissipation; but be filled with the Spirit"

1 John 3:17
"But whoever has this world's goods, and sees his brother in need, and shuts up his heart from him, how does the love of God abide in him?"

1 John 4:12
"No one has seen God at any time. If we love one another, God abides in us, and His love has been perfected in us."

Big Idea

The Holy Spirit is always in us, but He's not always filling us.

Materials

Tall, clear drinking glass, bottle or pitcher of milk, chocolate syrup, spoon.

Overview

It's such a hard thing to grasp. According to 1 Cor. 12:13, Romans 8:9, and Colossians 1:27, the Spirit of God is *in* every Christian. Yet though He is *in* us, He may not be filling us. In order to fill us, He must enlarge the capacity of our hearts for Him. In fact, that may be the primary purpose for our lives on this earth once He comes into our lives: to enlarge the capacity of our hearts for more of Him. And as we open ourselves to more of Him, the capacity of our hearts for *love* will be expanded. Therefore we must "work out our salvation with fear and trembling;" for, indeed, "It is God who is at work in you, both to will and to work for His good pleasure" (Philippians 2:12-13).

Sermon

How many of you like chocolate milk? What do you need in order to make chocolate milk? [A glass, milk, and chocolate. After they answer, pull the components out of a bag.] *I love chocolate milk! I think I'm going to make me some!* [At this point, pour the milk into the glass; then squeeze the chocolate syrup and let it fall into the milk; it will fall to the bottom. Pour a lot of chocolate in – which will evoke some laughs from the adults (and desire on the part of the kids). Then, take a sip of the milk.] *Hey, wait a minute! This doesn't taste like chocolate milk to me! I don't get it! I poured all that chocolate into the milk, but it doesn't taste like chocolate milk! What's the problem?* [Kids should yell out, "You need to stir it up!"] *Oh! You mean that even though the chocolate is in there, you can't taste it until it gets stirred into the milk? OK. Let me stir it.* [Stir it up.] *Let me try it now* [Drink the glass of chocolate milk; I like to down the whole glass – which really makes this funny.] *Ahhh! Now that's good chocolate milk! That chocolate reminds me of the Holy Spirit. The Bible says that the Holy Spirit lives in every Christian – but He doesn't always fill us. The Holy Spirit fills us when we let Him be stirred in us – by opening our hearts to others and loving them. Then the love of God fills our hearts – and the Holy Spirit fills us!*

Prayer

Lord, please fill our hearts with Your Spirit – so that You can be more fully released in us through love. Help us not to be stingy with Your love. May You be more and more released within us. In Jesus' name, Amen.

Church of Many Hats

Scripture

Matthew 5:44-47
"But I say to you, love your enemies, bless those who curse you, do good to those who hate you, and pray for those who spitefully use you and persecute you, that you may be sons of your Father in heaven . . . For if you love those who love you, what reward have you? Do not even the tax collectors do the same? And if you greet your friends only, what do you do more than the others?"

Romans 10:12
"For there is no distinction between Jew and Greek, for the same Lord over all is rich to all who call upon Him."

Big Idea

Loving those who are different reveals the heart and love of God.

Materials

Various hats or head-dresses from various countries (I used a hat from China, a yarmulke from Israel, and a kefia from Jordan)

Overview

The heart of the Father is one who reaches out toward the *other* – toward that which is different. Jesus teaches us that it's easy to love those who love you, who greet you, who think like you and look like you and talk like you. Everybody does that – including the "tax collectors" (in today's language, perhaps we could insert "terrorists?"). But to love someone who is different is more difficult. It requires movement and risk on our part – stepping out of our comfort zones. And to love our enemies requires even more – a level of sacrifice that reflects the cross. Yet in loving like that, we reveal the heart of our Father in heaven. This is the kind of love that changes the world.

Sermon

[I began by wearing a "Beijing 2008 Olympics" cap.] *"As you can see, I'm wearing a hat today."* A child yelled out, "Hey – I thought you're not supposed to wear hats in church! *"What kind of hat is this? Can anyone tell me where it's from?"* A couple children yelled out, "Beijing!" *"Does anyone know where Beijing is located?"* "China!" *"Yes, in China – and in China what language do they speak?"* "Chinese!" At this point I started saying a few phrases in Mandarin Chinese (*e.g.* *"Ni hao ma?"* – which means, "How are you?"*)

I then took out a yarmulke. *"Does anyone know what this is?"* The following are actual responses. One child yelled out, "A small shower cap!" Another blurted out, "A pope hat!" Then a little girl offered, "A yamaha!" The congregation was lost in laughter at this point. *"Well, you're getting close . . . it's actually called a yarmulke. Does anyone know what country this is from?"* At this, a little boy yelled out, "New York!" (Honestly, I am not making this up.) *"Well, yes, I'm sure there are many in New York who wear yarmulkes . . . but actually I got this in Israel. Does anyone know what language they speak in Israel?"* One girl yelled out "Swedish!" *"No, actually they speak Hebrew."* I then recited Deuteronomy 6:4 in Hebrew: *"Shema y'Israel: Adonai Elohenu, Adonai echad!"*

"Now I have one more headpiece I'm going to wear – and no, it's not an Italian tablecloth!" At this point I took out a red colored Arab kefia. *"Does anyone know what this is called?"* One girl said, "A towel!" Another said, "A turban!" *"Actually, it's called a kefia. Does anyone know what country this is from? This kind of headdress is worn in a lot of countries, especially in the Middle East. I got this one from Jordan. Do you know what language they speak in Jordan? They speak Arabic. Do you want to learn something in Arabic? Repeat after me: "Allah"* (They repeated.) *"Beehibuk"* (They repeated.) *"That means, 'God loves you!' Now let me ask you, do you think it bothers God that people are so different and that they dress so differently and speak so many different languages?"* "No!" *"No! Of course not! God loves the differences among us – He loves variety! Yet often I think we stay away from those who are different from us – who dress differently from us or who speak differently from us or who act differently from us. We become afraid of them. But Jesus said, if you only greet those (i.e. if you hang out with those) who are your friends – i.e. those who look like you and speak like you and think like you – what's the big deal with that? Everybody does that! But*

when you love someone who is very different from you, it's then that you are loving like God loves – it is then that you are like Jesus.

Prayer

Lord, help us to love those who are different from us – so that we might be like You, Jesus. Amen.

Clay

Scripture

Genesis 2:7
"And the Lord God formed man of the dust of the ground, and breathed into his nostrils the breath of life, and man became a living being"

Psalm 40:2
"He also brought me up out of a horrible pit, out of miry clay, and set my feet upon a rock"

Jeremiah 18:4-6
"And the vessel that he made of clay was marred in the hand of the potter; so he made it again into another vessel, as it seemed good to the potter to make. Then the word of the Lord came to me, saying, 'O house of Israel, can I not do with you as this potter?' says the Lord. 'Look, as the clay is in the potter's hand, so are you in My hand, O house of Israel!'"

Isaiah 64:8
"But now, O Lord, You are our Father; we are the clay, and You our potter; and we are the work of Your hand."

2 Corinthians 4:7
"But we have this treasure in earthen vessels, that the excellence of the power may be of God and not of us."

Big Idea

God desires for us to trust Him as a good potter when He shapes us and forms us and fires us into a beautiful vessel so He can fill us with Himself.

Materials

Soft clay (any arts & crafts store will have molding clay; or you can make your own – recipes abound on the Internet); finished pottery cup.

Overview

It is a fascinating thing to watch a potter at work. They take a lump of clay and pound it; they put it on a wheel and "throw" it, they shape it, mold it, sprinkle it with water, and then subject it to fire. The result is a thing of beauty – but it did not come without great labor and "pain." And God's desire is to make vessels of clay so that He, Himself might fill us with His very presence; but He can't fill us if we are already filled – with ourselves. And so we need to be emptied – so that He might fill us.

Sermon

I've got something with me today. (Hold up the clay.) *Do you know what this is?* (Clay!) *You know, I need to tell you: I like this clay. In fact, I love this clay. I'm just crazy about it. Now what would you think of me if I did this to my clay?* (At this point, rip off a piece of the clay and begin pounding it and kneading it and smashing it; then shape it into a ball, then push your thumbs into the center and begin to shape and form a cup or a vessel which could hold liquid.) *And what would you think of me if I then took this clay and put it into a fire and heated it up? Would you think I was mean to my clay? But what if, after all this, I took the clay out of the fire, and it produced this?* (At this point take out a finished pottery cup) *Isn't this beautiful? But the only way this could become so beautiful is if the potter pounded it and shaped it and formed it and then fired it. Who does the clay remind you of?* [A few of the kids said "Jesus," to which I said, "No – that usually works but not today!" But then a few of the kids said, "Us."] *Yes, this does remind me of us. The Bible says that God is the potter, and we are His clay. And He's making us into something beautiful – kind of like this cup with a hole in it – so that He can fill us with His very own presence! But in order to make us like this, He has to empty ourselves of "ourselves," so that He can fill us. But often this is a painful process. Ever feel like that clay? Ever feel like you're being pounded, or put in a fiery trial? When you feel that way, I want you to remember this clay. God loves us and is shaping us and forming us into something beautiful. But we have to trust Him while He's doing this to us.*

Prayer

Lord, You are the potter; we are Your clay. Mold us and make us into something beautiful – even if it hurts. And help us to trust You – even when it hurts – because You are a good potter – and You love us and want to fill us with Yourself. Amen.

Clockmaker

Scripture

Romans 1:20
"For since the creation of the world His invisible attributes are clearly seen, being understood by the things that are made, even His eternal power and Godhead, so that they are without excuse."

Psalm 14:1
"The fool has said in his heart, 'There is no God.'"

Big Idea

Just as a clock testifies to a clockmaker, the universe testifies to a Creator.

Materials

An inexpensive, plastic wall clock; shoebox.

Overview

People often describe those who believe in God as "people of faith," whereas people who don't believe in God (e.g. atheists) are almost assumed to be lacking faith. However, to look at the intricacies of the universe, or the human body, or of a fine piece of art, or the intricacies of matter at the subatomic level, and to see the order, beauty, and design, one quickly realizes that to believe that such order and design and beauty happened by "random chance" requires much faith. Just as a watch betrays a watchmaker, or a novel betrays an author, or a piece of art betrays an artist, so does our intricate and beautiful universe betray a Creator.

Sermon

[Beforehand, take apart the clock and put all the parts into the shoebox – the face, the cover, the minute hand, second hand, batteries, motor, etc.] *Good morning! I was thinking that I'd like to make a clock today! My old clock broke so I thought it would be cool to make a clock. So, I went shopping yesterday and I got all the parts to make a clock – the second hand, the minute hand, some batteries, a motor, the numbers, everything you need to make a clock! So I've got them all here in this shoebox . . . so let's make a clock!* [Cover the shoebox with the lid and then begin violently shaking the box for about ten seconds.] *Okay, it should be ready by now . . . let's take a look! Oh no! What's wrong! You know, I think I know what the problem is: I just didn't give it enough time! Maybe this time I should shake it a little longer.* [Shake the box this time for about twenty seconds.] *Okay, it should definitely have worked this time – let's take a look! Oh no! It's still not a clock! Maybe I need to give it a LOT more time. What if I shook the box for sixty seconds – do you think it would become a clock then?* [The kids yelled out, "NO!"] *What about sixty minutes? What about sixty days? What about sixty years – would it become a clock by then? What about six thousand years? Or six million years? Or six billion years? Or six gazillion years? Would it become a clock then?* [NO!] *Well, what's the problem? What do I need to do?* ["You need someone to put it together!] *"Oh! So what you're telling me is that in order to have a clock, you need a clockmaker, right? Okay, then let me ask you this. How did this beautiful world come into existence? Did it "just happen" by chance?* [No!] *Of course not! Just as a clock tells us that there must have been a clockmaker, so the world tells us that Someone must have made it – that it couldn't have just "happened by chance." Who made the world? That's right – the answer to every children's sermon: JESUS!*

Prayer

Lord thank You for this beautiful world, and our beautiful and amazing bodies, which tell us that Someone had a beautiful design and plan for us. Thank you for making us, and all the universe, for us to enjoy. Amen.

Connected Body Parts

Scripture

1 Corinthians 12:12-27
"Now you are the body of Christ,
and members individually."

Big Idea

If body parts aren't connected, it's not a body.

Materials

Mr. Potato Head with body parts, bag, bucket.

Overview

Corporate worship brings everyone together – to pray together, to worship together, and to be edified by each other's stories and testimonies together. As our church grew larger, we increasingly saw the need for more opportunities for body life to be displayed (we introduced a monthly mid-week "body life" service with this in mind – where we allow ample time for corporate prayer, sharing, and testimonies). We came to realize that many in our body were doing beautiful, creative kinds of ministry in their own spheres of influence (not necessarily in or through the "institutional" church). The problem was, we just weren't aware of it. We agreed that it was important to find out what was going on in the body (stuff that a lot of folks did "in secret") and to *celebrate* it together – thereby bringing encouragement and joy to the entire body of Christ as we could all see what Jesus was doing in our midst.

Sermon

Begin holding brown paper bag with Mr. Potato parts in it; have a small bucket nearby. *Imagine for a minute that I was God, and I wanted to make a human body. If I wanted to make a body, what would I need?* [One child responded, "Power!"] *I'd need body parts! So what would you need?* At this point, kids will start shouting out body parts – e.g. hands, eyes, ears, feet, etc. [For humor, one of the other pastors shouted out "spleen!"] As they say the body part, take it out of the bag in drop it into the bucket. When all the parts are in the bucket, then say, *"OK – here's the body!*

At this point, reach into the bucket and grab all the body parts and hold them up in your hands. *Here's my body!* [Look distressed.] *What's wrong? What's the matter?* (The body parts aren't connected!) Begin assembling together all the body parts on Mr. Potato Head. *You see, a body is not a body if it's not connected together! And that's how it is with us – the Body of Christ! If one part of the body is off doing its own thing, it's not connected with the body and is not a part of the body. Jesus wants and needs all of us – each of us has unique gifts that we have to offer to the body. But we always need to remember: if the body parts aren't connected, then we're not a body.*

Prayer

Lord, thank You for all the individual members of our body. Help us to recognize and appreciate *all* the different, unique parts that make us who we are. Help us to celebrate each other and what You are doing uniquely through each of us – and how You bring us all together for Your glory. Amen.

Couch Potato

Scripture

Matthew 16:24-25

"Then Jesus said to His disciples, 'If anyone desires to come after Me, let him deny himself, and take up his cross, and follow Me. For whoever desires to save his life will lose it, but whoever loses his life for My sake will find it.'"

Psalm 116:15-17

"Precious in the sight of the Lord is the death of His saints. O Lord, truly I am Your servant; I am Your servant, the son of Your maidservant; You have loosed my bonds. I will offer to You the sacrifice of thanksgiving, and will call upon the name of the Lord."

John 12:27-28

"Now My soul is troubled, and what shall I say? 'Father, save Me from this hour?' But for this purpose I came to this hour. Father, glorify Your name." Then a voice came from heaven, saying, 'I have both glorified it and will glorify it again.'"

Big Idea

We fulfill our design when we sacrifice – like Jesus.

Materials

One "old" potato – which has started to sprout roots and beginning to become soft.

Overview

A potato that is not used (i.e. "sacrificed") will fail to fulfill its purpose for existence (to be eaten and enjoyed). A potato must "lose its life" to fulfill its purpose – in the form of mashed potatoes, baked potatoes, French fries – whereby it becomes pleasing and satisfying to its owner. If it is not sacrificed and used, it begins to rot and fails to be of any use to its owner. In the same way, when we hold onto our life – protecting it, conserving it, saving it – we end up losing it, and are of little use to our Owner. But when we sacrifice and lay down our lives, we become a "pleasing aroma" to our Father in heaven – Who sees images of His Son in us when we sacrifice and love.

Sermon

What is this I'm holding? [A potato.] *Yes, but there's something unusual about this potato, isn't there? What is it?* [It's got hair growing on it!] *That's right. Now how did that happen? It starts growing stuff on it when it's not being used . . . when it's sitting in the cupboard – or sitting on a couch* ☺ *. And if I left this potato alone for, say, another week or two, what would happen to the potato?* [It would begin to rot!] *Then is it any use to me?* [No!] *Why did God create potatoes?* [To eat them!] *So what do I need to do to this potato before it begins to rot and becomes useless to me?* [You need to eat it!] *I need to cut it up – because then I can boil it and mash it, put a little butter and salt and pepper on it – and then I can enjoy some yummy mashed potatoes. Or I can cut it up in strips and deep fry it, and then I can enjoy some delicious French Fries. But in order for any of this to happen, what needs to happen to this potato?* [It needs to be cut up!] *Yes – it needs to be sacrificed! In order for a potato to fulfill its purpose, it needs to be sacrificed. Now, who owns us?* [God.] *Why did He create us?* [To sacrifice.] *Yes – when we give ourselves away, and love others, and sacrifice our lives, we become very pleasing to God.*

Prayer

Lord thank You for Jesus, who showed us that the greatest joy in life is when we sacrifice our lives for others. Help us to trust You when we sacrifice our lives – to really know and believe that You are pleased when we do this – and we'll really find our lives. Amen.

Covering

Scripture

James 1:27
"Pure and undefiled religion before God and the Father is this: to visit orphans and widows in their trouble, and to keep oneself unspotted from the world."

Isaiah 1:16b-17
"Cease to do evil, learn to do good; seek justice, rebuke the oppressor; defend the fatherless, plead for the widow."

Psalm 146:9
"The Lord watches over the strangers; He relieves the fatherless and widow . . ."

Acts 2:44-45
"Now all who believed were together, and had all things in common, and sold their possessions and goods, and divided them among all, as anyone had need."

Big Idea

When the church provides a covering for widows and orphans, it reflects God's heart.

Materials

Umbrella, piece of roofing material (asphalt shingle).

Overview

A famous French philosopher once said that a society will be judged by the way it treats those who are least able to care for themselves. The Bible is filled with pictures and stories and words which detail God's passionate concern for the most vulnerable in society — widows, orphans, and the stranger. In Luke 7, Luke records that Jesus' heart was moved when he saw the only son of a widow being led out in a funeral procession in Nain — and He healed him and gave him back to his mother (who would have been left destitute and at the mercy of others). At the crucifixion, Jesus' last words of instruction were given to His friend John, instructing him to care for Mary, His mother — who evidently was a widow at that point (and it's interesting that Jesus' brother James was nowhere to be found at the crucifixion — though years later he penned his famous words in James 1:27). One of the greatest opportunities given to the church to reflect the Father's heart is how it responds to opportunities to care for "the least of these."

Sermon

[Hold up an umbrella.] *Who knows what this is? Yes, it's an umbrella. What does an umbrella do?* [Several kids answered, "It keeps you dry."] *Yes, it keeps you dry – but what else does it do?* [One girl answered, "It covers you."] *Yes! An umbrella provides a covering. It protects you from rain, or snow, or the sun. So when you're under the umbrella, you're covered and protected.* [Move the umbrella over some of the kids.] *Now let me show you something else* [Show them the asphalt shingle.] *Does anyone know what this is?* [One girl answered, "Sandpaper!"] *That's a pretty good guess, but it's not sandpaper.* [A boy shouted out, "Construction material!"] *Yes, it's construction material – but what kind of construction material?* [The same boy said, "Roofing material!"] *Yes, it's roofing material. Do you know what this roofing material is called? It's called a shingle. What does a shingle do? It covers and protects your roof. So what do these two things have in common?* [They both cover things.] *Yes, they both cover and protect things. This reminds me of the church. Not this building, but us – we are the church. Who does the church protect?* [Some kids said "us!"] *Yes, but the Bible makes a point to say that the church especially protects people in need – like widows and orphans and the fatherless. Isn't that beautiful? That's God's heart – He loves the widow and the orphan and the stranger. So when we cover and protect those who don't have a family, we show the world God's heart.*

Prayer

Lord, thank You for Your heart, which loves the widow and the orphan. Thank You for Your church, and for the opportunity to reflect Your heart. Amen.

Cracked Pots for Christ

Scripture

2 Corinthians 4:6-7

"For it is the God who commanded light to shine out of darkness, who has shone in our hearts to give the light of the knowledge of the glory of God in the face of Jesus Christ. But we have this treasure in earthen vessels, that the excellence of the power may be of God and not of us."

Big Idea

God shines His light brightest through our weaknesses.

Materials

Clay flower pot with tray (carefully chisel a crack on one side of the pot), bright light (mechanic's light with cord is best).

Overview

This idea of God's glory and power being displayed through earthen vessels is the heart of the New Covenant ("Christ in you, the hope of Glory" – Colossians 1:27). It is the essence of our calling ("But when it pleased God, who separated me from my mother's womb and called me through His grace, to reveal His Son in me . . ." Galatians 1: 15-16). And it is an incredibly *hopeful* message to broken vessels like us.

Sermon

Display clay pot, using the bottom tray as a lid. Have crack away from the kids at first so they can't see it.

Ask: *What is this I'm holding?* (Clay pot.) *Some people call this an "earthen vessel." Why would they call it that?* (Because it's made out of the earth – the ground.)

    Now suppose the potter formed this earthen vessel from the dust of the ground, and then he wanted to put a light inside of it (insert light inside the clay pot), *then he sealed the pot so that the light would always be inside.* [Put clay tray on top, sealing in the light as best you can.] *Can you see the light?* (No.) *But the potter wants people to see the light inside . . . but you can't see it. How will we be able to see the light?* [At this point, one child spoke out: "It needs to be broken!"] *Maybe we need to look for some weaknesses – for some cracks.* [Turn the pot around – so the kids can now see the side with the crack.] *Can you see the light now?* (Yes!) *So, you can see the light where the clay pot was cracked . . . where it was weak! Now, who does this remind you of?* [Some of the children said "Jesus!" to which I responded, "Well, that will usually work . . . but not today! This produced laughter from the adults.]

Answer: *It reminds me of us! The Bible says that we're "earthen vessels" and God has put His light in us! A lot of the time we think that when we're weak, God can't shine His light through us . . . but really, it is when we are weak that God is most able to shine His light though us – just like this cracked, clay pot. So do you know what that makes us? Cracked pots for Christ!*

Prayer

Lord, thank You that Your light resides in us and is sealed in us – and will always be in us. So help us to be grateful, Jesus, for the cracks in our lives – our wounds, our weaknesses, our struggles – which provide a place for You to be strong where we are so weak. In Your name, Amen.

Easter Hope

Scripture

Revelation 21:5
"Then, He who sat on the throne said, 'Behold, I make all things new.' And He said to me, 'Write, for these words are faithful and true.'"

John 11:25
"Jesus said to her, 'I am the resurrection and the life. He who believes in Me, though he may die, he shall live.'"

Romans 6:5
"For if we have been united together in the likeness of His death, certainly we also shall be in the likeness of His resurrection."

1 Corinthians 15:51-53
"Behold, I tell you a mystery: We shall not all sleep, but we shall all be changed – in a moment, in the twinkling of an eye, at the last trumpet. For the trumpet will sound, and the dead will be raised incorruptible, and we shall be changed. For this corruptible must put on incorruption, and this mortal must put on immortality."

Big Idea

Jesus makes all things new!

Materials

You will need to find a video of a chrysalis – which captures the significant moments of transformation – e.g. when the caterpillar morphs into a chrysalis, and then when the butterfly emerges. These are easy to find on the internet (e.g. on *YouTube*). Our media person found two short videos which he edited together for this.

Overview

When I officiate at funerals, I sometimes close the service by sharing the idea that in order for there to be a birth into one world, there has to be a death in another world. Think about your birth into this world. You're in this womb-world where it's hard to imagine there's anything else. You're fed, you're warm. And yet, there are some things that don't make sense: You've got these hands . . . what are they for? You've got these feet? What are they for? And a nose for smelling and ears for hearing. They're hints, reminders that you're not meant for this (womb) world, but for another. And then the time comes: and there's labor, and people are gathered 'round, and there's blood and sweat, and heavy breathing, and then you begin the transition from one world into the next . . . and then all of a sudden, the world which you knew for 9 short months is now behind, and there's great rejoicing on the other side. *You've been born into the world for which you were made all along.* The video of the chrysalis illustrates this beautifully, and it points to the hope of the resurrection – which we celebrate on Easter!

Sermon

Say: *Hey everyone – check this out! I want you to watch the video screen and I'm going to show you something.* [Show video of chrysalis. This is really a beautiful and stunning thing to watch, and it evoked oohs and ahhs from the kids and even from among the adults.] *Does anyone know what this is?* [I got a lot of varied responses, but eventually someone said "chrysalis."] *Isn't that cool? At first, it looked like the caterpillar was dead, didn't it? It looked like its life was over. But was its life over? Well, as a caterpillar, its life was coming to an end. But then what happened? Its life was changed – it was transformed into something else – into a beautiful caterpillar which was alive – and which could fly! Isn't that cool how God does that? I think God created things like caterpillars and butterflies to show us how the death of one life can be transformed into a new life – that's even more beautiful. Who does that remind you of?* [Everyone yelled, JESUS!!!] *You got it! That's what we're celebrating today on Easter: Jesus has risen from the dead! And it also reminds me of us – for that's kind of what God is doing and will do in our lives – transforming our mortal lives into something beautiful that will live forever! Let's pray!*

Prayer

Father thank you for the new life we have in Jesus! Thank you for raising Jesus from the dead, and how He is a "first fruits" to show us what You are doing in our lives. We trust You, Jesus, and we trust that You are transforming us from these mortal bodies of death into glorious children who will live and reign forever with You! Amen!

Exposed in the Light

Scripture

Ephesians 5:8-14
"For you were once darkness, but now you are light in the Lord. Walk as children of light (for the fruit of the Spirit is in all goodness, righteousness, and truth), finding out what is acceptable to the Lord. And have no fellowship with the unfruitful works of darkness, but rather expose them. For it is shameful even to speak of those things which are done by them in secret. But all things that are exposed are made manifest by the light, for whatever makes manifest is light. Therefore He says: 'Awake, you who sleep, Arise from the dead, and Christ will give you light.'"

Psalm 32:1-5
"Blessed is he whose transgression is forgiven, whose sin is covered. Blessed is the man to whom the Lord does not impute iniquity, and in whose spirit there is no deceit. When I kept silent, my bones grew old through my groaning all the day long. For day and night Your hand was heavy upon me; My vitality was turned into the drought of summer. I acknowledged my sin to You, and my iniquity I have not hidden. I said, 'I will confess my transgressions to the Lord,' and You forgave the iniquity of my sin."

1 John 1:7
"But if we walk in the light as He is in the light, we have fellowship with one another, and the blood of Jesus Christ His Son cleanses us from all sin."

Materials
Small potted plant (which is wilting, dying); towel.

Big Idea
Hiding our sin in the dark leads to death; but exposing our sin in the light leads to life.

Overview

Any child knows that a plant kept in darkness, even though watered and fertilized, will eventually wilt and die due to lack of exposure to the light. So it is with us and our sins. As long as we keep our sins hidden and submerged, we will wilt under its weight, leaving only bondage and fear. But when we confess our sin and bring it into the light of His grace, it is no longer ours to bear – but His. And His light transforms it into light itself. This truth is easy to grasp with our head; yet it is one of the most difficult things to believe and be convinced of in our hearts. And it leads to much heartache and suffering.

Sermon

[Bring out potted plant with a towel over it and show it to the children]. *I've got this plant, and I'm having trouble with it and I need your help. It's wilting and dying, and I don't know what is wrong.*

[Lift off the towel to reveal the wilting and dying plant.] *I've watered it and I've fertilized it, and I've kept it well covered by this towel, and have kept it from being exposed to the light. For I didn't want it to be exposed to any light where it might get hurt by it. But now look at it: it's wilting and looks terrible, and it's dying. What did I do wrong?* [At this the children all raised their hands and were quick to point out the error of my ways.] *You mean to tell me that the plant actually needs to be exposed to the light? You mean keeping it in the darkness, hidden from the light, will actually cause it to wilt and die? Well, of course you all are right . . . keeping a living plant from being exposed to the light will indeed cause it to wilt and die – that's actually pretty obvious, isn't it? Yet as crazy as that sounds, that reminds me of how a lot of us think about our sins! All of us sin, right? Yet when we sin, we have a choice: we can hide our sin and keep it hidden and in the darkness, or we can confess our sin and bring it into the light and receive God's forgiveness and grace!*

Have you ever sinned, and then you kept it a secret? What was that like – what did you feel like inside? Yes – you were probably burdened with guilt and shame. And sometimes we're terrified of admitting our sin and confessing it – yet this is the very thing that will give us freedom. Because the Bible says that when we confess our sin and bring it into the light, it actually becomes light! Isn't that cool? Let's pray.

Prayer

Father, thank You for Your grace, which frees us up from hiding from our sin in shame; and thank You that when we confess our sin and bring it into Your light, it becomes light. Amen.

Extreme Love

Scripture

Romans 5:7-8
"For scarcely for a righteous man will one die; yet perhaps for a good man someone would even dare to die. But God demonstrates His own love toward us, in that while we were still sinners, Christ died for us."

James 2:26
"For as the body without the spirit is dead, so faith without works is dead also."

Big Idea

Extreme faith produces extreme love in a world that is dark and obsessed with fairness.

Materials

Rappelling equipment (ropes, gloves, harness, etc.), shorts, hiking boots, sunglasses, bandana, T-shirt.

Overview

This children's sermon was actually a "promo" for a children's Vacation Bible School program at our church. The theme was "Extreme Love." Love is a concept that is quite muddled in our society. The greatest demonstration of love, as Paul says in Romans 5, is that one would sacrifice for another. That is the ultimate mark of love. But in order to experience God's "extreme love," we need to have "extreme faith" to believe He could actually love us that much – and to believe that He is actually *that* powerful and *that* good. Here in Colorado, "X-treme" sports are very prevalent, such as rappelling. Thus the idea for this children's sermon was born. We also have a very large, strong cross up on a stage, both of which were needed to make this sermon possible.

Sermon

[I ran out on stage dressed in "X-treme" outdoor gear – with a bandana around my head, hiking boots, khaki shorts, and sunglasses. I played the part and shouted out the words of this in a "dude" kind of way.] *Yo – kids – how 'ya doin'? I'm in an EXTREME kind of mood this morning – I got up EXTREMELY early and had an EXTREME protein breakfast and got on my EXTREME equipment . . . I'm ready for something EXTREME! Are you ready for something EXTREME? Let me ask you, "How much does God love us?" That's right – you got it: EXTREMELY! But we need to believe that He loves us – and the proof of that will be how much we're willing to EXTREMELY LOVE – for if we really believe and trust that He loves us, we'll love others the way He loves us! We'll be willing to take risks and trust Him and trust His love. So I'm going to do something EXTREME! I've got me some rappelling equipment and do you know what I'm going to do? I'm going to rappel off this stage!* [At this point I secured my rappelling equipment to a rope, which was secured around the base of the large cross on the stage. I then backed up to the edge of the stage and began to rappel down the stage, the rope being held by the cross. As I hung over the edge before going down, I then said the following.] *Now, I bet a lot of you are wondering: Can a big, sinful guy like me trust this cross to support me when I jump off this cliff?* At this point many yelled out, *"Yes!"* and then I rappelled down off the stage. *You can trust that cross – you can trust in Jesus' love to sustain you when you sacrifice your life for others. That's EXTREME faith in His EXTREME love!*

Prayer

Lord, thank You that we can trust in Your goodness and power – and in Your extreme love for us – which releases us and frees us up to take risks and love others – extremely! In Your name, Amen.

Eye of the Hurricane

Scripture

Psalm 107:23-31

"Those who go down to the sea in ships, who do business on great waters, they see the works of the Lord, and His wonders in the deep. For He commands and raises the stormy wind, which lifts up the waves of the sea. They mount up to the heavens, they go down again to the depths; Their soul melts because of trouble. They reel to and fro, and stagger like a drunken man, and are at their wits' end. Then they cry out to the Lord, and He brings them out of their distresses. He calms the storm, so that its waves are still. Then they are glad because they are quiet; so He guides them to their desired haven. Oh that men would give thanks to the Lord for His goodness, and for His wonderful works to the children of men!"

Luke 8:23-24

"But as they sailed He fell asleep. And a windstorm came down on the lake, and they were filling with water, and were in jeopardy. And they came to Him and awoke Him saying, 'Master, Master, we are perishing!' Then He arose and rebuked the wind and the raging of the water. And they ceased, and there was a calm."

Hebrews 13:5-6

"Let your conduct be without covetousness; be content with such things as you have. For He Himself has said, 'I will never leave you nor forsake you.' So we may boldly say, 'The Lord is my helper; I will not fear. What can man do to me?"

Psalm 23:4

"Yea, though I walk through the valley of the shadow of death, I will fear no evil; for You are with me."

Big Idea

Jesus is with us in the midst of the storm.

Materials

You will need a really good satellite photo of a hurricane. I did this children's sermon one week after the Hurricane Katrina; so I got a satellite photo off the Internet and had it projected onto the video screen. You can usually find some good photos on the NOAA/National Weather Service web site; here's a link to one: http://antwrp.gsfc.nasa.gov/apod/ap050829.html. If you don't have a video screen, try to make a copy of a photo on an overhead projector, or find a large print photo.

Overview

It was Labor Day weekend, 2005, and I was ready to do a children's sermon on "Labor Day." But the entire United States was reeling from the impact of Hurricane Katrina, which brought devastation to New Orleans and much of the Louisiana, Mississippi, and Alabama coastline. We decided late in the week to change what we had planned for the services and dedicated the entire service to addressing the impact of the catastrophic storm, and our response to it. Being a former meteorologist, I had always been fascinated by hurricanes, but I was especially intrigued by the eye of a hurricane. Such clear and calm in the middle of pure hell on earth. Katrina had one of the most well-defined eyes I had ever seen – almost 30 miles across.

I chatted with a friend just before the service who was enduring a "storm" of her own. She had been assaulted in a hospital while medicated and being treated for terminal cancer. Now, a few years later, having suffered indignity after indignity from lawyers and doctors (though amazingly still alive!), she had discovered just a few days earlier that her court trial would be postponed yet again – perhaps for months. She saw no way out of the vortex God had placed her in. So many times she had wanted to run. But she told me she had begun to find some peace and clarity through His presence in the midst of her hell. I was stunned; and I looked in her eyes and said, "This children's sermon is for you." When I began the children's sermon and we projected the photo of the massive storm with its clearly defined eye, you could sense the awe and sobriety in the congregation. Jesus never promised to keep us from tribulation and storms. But sometimes we need to lean into these very storms to see that Jesus was (and is) there – right in its very midst, providing a sense of transcendent calm and clarity in the midst of the storm.

Sermon

I want to show you something. [We showed a satellite photo of Hurricane Katrina on the video screen.] *Do any of you know what this is?* [At one of our services, the children were all very young – and they didn't know what it was. One child yelled out, "The Milky Way!" which I thought was a pretty good answer for someone who had probably never seen a satellite photo of a hurricane. Most of the older kids recognized the photo instantly.] *This is a picture of Hurricane Katrina, taken from space. Pretty amazing, huh? This photo was taken last Sunday, just before it struck the United States. Look at how big the storm was! Can you imagine the winds in this storm? If you look at the outside edge of the storm, the winds there are probably around 10-20 MPH. As you move closer to the center, the winds pick up to around 50-60 MPH; then as you move closer they're up around 100 MPH; but if you move even closer to the center, they're up around 160 MPH! And then, if you get right in the very center of the storm, it's there that you'll find the strongest winds of all! Right?* [Several of the kids shouted out, "No!"] *Those of you who said "No" are correct. Because what is it like in the center of the storm – in the "eye" of the hurricane?* [One child yelled out, "There's no wind!"] *Exactly! Isn't that amazing? That in the center of this powerful storm with 160 MPH winds, it is perfectly calm and clear!*

Do you know what that reminds me of? Our life with Jesus. Because sometimes we have our own "storms" in life. Sometimes hard things happen to us – maybe you get sick; or maybe you had a parent or a grandparent who is very sick – or maybe they even died. Or maybe you are having some family problems right now. [Note: a few weeks prior to this, I had done a water baptism where nine of the twelve people I baptized were kids between the ages of eight and thirteen. And of these nine, five of them referred to "family problems" when testifying of Jesus' presence in their lives. Indeed, young children are not immune from "storms."] *The Bible doesn't promise us that hard times won't come; but it does promise us that Jesus will be with us in the midst of the storm! In fact, sometimes this is where you can see Jesus the best – when you are suffering in the midst of a terrible storm in your life.*

Prayer

Lord Jesus, thank You that you never leave us nor forsake us. Thank You for being right there with us in the midst of our own storms. Help us to trust You. Thank You for the calm and the clarity You provide as we look to You in the midst of our storms. Amen.

Father's Day

Scripture

Genesis 1:27
"So God created man in His own image, in the image of God He created him; male and female He created them."

Big Idea

We need to be grateful for both mommies and daddies (i.e. male and female), for together they help us better understand what God is like.

Materials

Electric shaver (or you can use a razor blade if you don't have one).

Overview

This children's sermon evoked one of the funniest responses from a child ever heard in our church. It was a Father's Day children's sermon, and I wanted to highlight the differences between "mommies and daddies" (i.e. male and female), and how both male and female are unique, and each help us understand something about the nature of God — in whose image we are made, male and female. I began by coming out on the stage while shaving myself with an electric razor, and asking the question, "How can you tell the difference between a mommy and a daddy?" I thought the electric shaver was a sure-fire giveaway to a "safe" answer.

Sermon

[I came out on the stage shaving my face with an electric shaver.] *How can you tell the difference between mommies and daddies?* [I let the kids give some answers, but I had planned to interject the following answers: "Daddies shave their faces; mommies shave their legs. Daddies wear ties; mommies wear dresses. Daddies like the 3 Stooges, Mommies don't," etc.] But while the kids were giving their answers, one little boy, in childlike straightforwardness and innocence, offered this distinction (with a booming voice, I might add): *"Moms have boobs!"* The congregations totally lost it! It took me nearly five minutes to get them back.

After pulling the congregation back together (which was no easy task), I then tried to get back to the sermon: *"So why do you think God made mommies and daddies different?"* (At this point I quickly answered my own question, fearing any further damage.) *"Is it bad that they're different? No! They both help us to understand what God is like. The Bible says that God is our Father. But the Bible also says that God cares for us the way a mother hen cares for her chicks (Luke 13:34); and the way a mother cares for the unborn baby in her belly (Isaiah 49:13-16). A few weeks ago we celebrated Mother's Day, and this week we're celebrating Father's Day. And that's great – we need to be thankful for both mommies and daddies, for they help us better understand what God is like. God loves us and protects us like a Father; but God also loves us and protects us like a Mother!*

*Important Note: I say in all sincerity that I did not anticipate that response. I say this because I think that's what truly made this funny. And I say this because it would be easy to set up children's sermons that are intentionally designed to evoke off-color responses, for the sake of a joke for the adults. There is a fine line between enjoying the children's innocent responses for a great laugh, and deliberately setting up the kids to make a stab at adult humor. We need to be cautious of crossing this line.

Prayer

Lord, thank You for mommies and for daddies. Thank You that each of them, in their own, unique way, help us to understand something about You. We pray that You would bless our mothers and our fathers today, and we especially thank You for our fathers on this Father's Day. And Lord please be with those who don't have a father here on this earth. Thank You that You are our true Father in heaven. Amen.

Fear and Love

Scripture

1 John 4:16-19
"And we have known and believed the love that God has for us. God is love, and he who abides in love abides in God, and God in him. Love has been perfected among us in this: that we may have boldness in the day of judgment; because as He is, so are we in this world. There is no fear in love; but perfect love casts out fear, because fear involves torment. But he who fears has not been made perfect in love. We love Him because He first loved us."

2 Timothy 1:7
"For God has not given us a spirit of fear, but of power and of love and of a sound mind."

Galatians 5:13-14
"For you, brethren, have been called to liberty; only do not use liberty as an opportunity for the flesh, but through love serve one another. For all the law is fulfilled in one word, even in this: 'You shall love your neighbor as yourself.'"

Big Idea

Perfect love casts out fear, so that we might love others the way God loves us.

Materials

Large ball
(to play catch)

Overview

A mentor once taught me that in order to best understand a word or concept, you need to know it's opposite (i.e. antonym). The Scriptures here seem to indicate that the opposite of fear is not so much courage, but rather it is *love*. This is an intriguing concept, as it reveals that fear in most cases may reveal a fixation or preoccupation with the self; and that the solution to overcoming fear is to become *other-centered*, as opposed to drumming up courage – which is still all about the self. Loving truly is liberating.

Sermon

[Note: The key to this sermon is to be very enthusiastic and expressive while you talk.] *I was thinking that it might be fun to play a game of catch with you all. I'm going to need some of you to help me. Can I get four or five volunteers?* [At this point I led the volunteers away from the other children and up to the stage.] *Are you ready to play catch? Catch is a fun game. Okay – let's play.* [Make like you're getting ready to pass the ball . . . but you just can't.] *I . . . I . . . I . . . I don't think I can do this . . . because if I play catch with you, you're going to get to know me, and once you get to know me you might make fun of my big nose or my balding head . . . I'm so afraid you might make fun of me so I don't think I can play.* [At this point one of the children said, with the most sincere and sweet voice, "We won't make fun of you"– which melted my heart along with most of the congregations'.] *Okay . . . you're right . . . you all are good kids so I shouldn't be afraid so let's play catch.* [Again make like you're ready to pass the ball; but again, you can't do it.] *I . . . I . . . I just can't do it! Because what if we play catch and I drop the ball? I'm so afraid I'll drop the ball . . . I just can't do this . . . I mean, what if I fail? I'm so afraid of failing, I just can't play.* [At this point one little girl said, "Don't worry, I can show you and teach you how to play," which again melted my heart; but I played off this answer.] *Yes – but that's just it . . . what if I learn to play and I DO catch the ball and I play good . . . then whenever we play, you will expect me to do good, and you'll have such high expectations of me – I just don't know if I can live up to those expectations.* [At this point, the congregation was laughing.] *I'm so afraid!!! Oh – you know what? Our time is up for the children's sermon. Let's go.* [At this point I led the children back down the stage where they joined the other kids; the congregation was really laughing at this point. Once they joined the other kids, I then talked to them.] *So, did you have a good time?* ["No!"] *You didn't? What was the problem?* [One of the kids, a latecomer, exclaimed, "I just got here!"] *Oh . . . but why did you kids who played catch not enjoy the game? What was the problem?* [A little girl spoke out, "You were too afraid!"] *Yes! I was too afraid! I was paralyzed by fear! The problem was that I was thinking only about myself. You know, the Bible says, "Perfect love casts out fear." That means that if I'm still afraid, it must mean I'm not receiving God's love for me – and I'm still plagued by fear. And when I'm plagued by fear, I think only about myself and I don't love others! I need Jesus to set me free from my "self"– so I can be freed up to love others.*

Prayer

Lord Jesus, help us to see those around us and love them, so that we might be freed up from fear. May Your perfect love cast out all our fears – so that we might love like You. Amen.

Feeder Fish

Scripture

John 12:24-25

"Most assuredly, I say to you, unless a grain of wheat falls into the ground and dies, it remains alone; but if it dies, it produces much grain. He who loves his life will lose it, and he who hates his life in this world will keep it for eternal life."

John 6:54-57

"Whoever eats My flesh and drinks My blood has eternal life, and I will raise him up on the last day. For My flesh is food indeed, and My blood is drink indeed. He who eats My flesh and drinks My blood abides in Me, and I in him. As the living Father sent Me, and I live because of the Father, so he who feeds on Me will live because of Me."

Big Idea

The way of Jesus is to sacrifice one's life so that others might live.

Materials

Two or three small "feeder" fish in a clear glass bowl. They are about a half inch in length, and cost less than a dollar apiece at most pet stores.

Overview

The message of the gospel is radically counter-cultural. In a society that is consumed with preserving one's own rights, and self-protection, Jesus' life points us in a far different direction: If we spend our lives trying to save our lives, we'll lose it. But if we will lay down our lives in trust and obedience to the Father, as Jesus did, it is there that we will find our lives. If "survival of the fittest" is the world's way, "death by the fittest" is the way of Jesus.

Sermon

I have something I want to show you. I went to the pet store yesterday and I got these. Do you know what they are? (Fish!) *Yes, but they are a certain kind of fish – they are very, very small – does anyone know what they're called? They are called "Feeder Fish." Can anyone tell me: What is the purpose of Feeder Fish? Why do they exist?* (Several said, "They feed on things.") *Actually, the purpose of Feeder Fish is that other, bigger fish feed on <u>them</u>! So think about it: The purpose of these fish, which are smaller than all other fish, is to die so that other fish might live. Now who does that remind you of?* (They all shouted out, Jesus!) *Yes! Jesus came to sacrifice His life, so that others might live. So, don't you want to be like Jesus?* (It was fascinating to watch their response when I asked this. Some initially shouted out "Yes"– but then you could see the look of ambivalence on their faces.) *I then said, "Well . . . sometimes I'm not so sure! Sometimes it's hard to be like Jesus. But isn't Jesus amazing: The whole reason for His life was to sacrifice Himself so that we might live!* [At this point, a little girl shouted out, "But these are only fish!" The entire congregation burst out laughing. I had to navigate my way through that one – describing how the fish were just meant to be a "picture" that *reminds* us of Jesus].

Prayer

Lord Jesus, You are amazing. Thank You for dying so that we might live. And help us to be like You – to live our lives for others, so that by our sacrifice others might live. In Your name, Amen.

Fruitfulness

Scripture

Galatians 5:22-26

"But the fruit of the Spirit is love, joy, peace, longsuffering, kindness, goodness, faithfulness, gentleness, self-control. Against such there is no law. And those who are Christ's have crucified the flesh with its passions and desires. If we live in the Spirit, let us also walk in the Spirit. Let us not become conceited, provoking one another, envying one another."

Colossians 1:27-29

"To them God willed to make known what are the riches of the glory of this mystery among the Gentiles: which is Christ in you, the hope of glory. Him we preach, warning every man and teaching every man in all wisdom, that we may present every man perfect in Christ Jesus. To this end I also labor, striving according to His working which works in me mightily."

John 15:5

"I am the vine, you are the branches. He who abides in Me, and I in him, bears much fruit; for without Me you can do nothing."

Romans 7:4

"Therefore, my brethren, you also have become dead to the law through the body of Christ, that you may be married to another – to Him who was raised from the dead, that we should bear fruit to God."

Materials

Pieces of fake (plastic or wooden) fruit, and corresponding real fruit.

Big Idea

Real fruit of the Spirit takes time, and is produced by the Spirit of God at work in our lives.

Overview

The Colossians text (listed above) gives us the paradox of our sanctification: i.e. that our growth and fruitfulness depends on our labor and striving – yet it's a striving that's not according to our own strength and resources, but a striving that's "according to His mighty power which is (already) at work in me." It's like a woman giving birth to a baby, knowing that she indeed had to work and labor to deliver this baby; but she marvels at the genesis that took place within her, knowing that this was far bigger than her. Indeed, her striving was "according to His working which works in me mightily." So it is with any and all fruit that we might bear for the kingdom. It all comes from the vine, and "apart from Me you can do nothing." Romans 7:4 says that the only way we can bear fruit is by union (literally "marriage") with Christ. Think about it: in the physical world, fruit can't be produced apart from the tree from which it came. Jesus hung on a tree, in order to produce great fruit – through His bride – the church.

Sermon

You know, everywhere in the Bible, God talks a lot about how we're supposed to "bear fruit" – e.g. "Be fruitful and multiply"and how we're supposed to produce the "Fruit of the Spirit." So I was thinking about this today, and I thought, I want to please God, so I'd better get on the ball and make some fruit! So, I went out in my garage, got my stuff together, and worked real hard all day, and now look what I have! [At this point, take the fake fruit out of the bag and show it to the kids.] *Isn't this great fruit! Doesn't it look beautiful? Isn't it colorful? I bet it's soooo delicious – 'cause fruit that looks this good surely tastes good, too!* [At this point, give out the fruit to the kids – ask them to eat it.] *What's the matter? Why aren't you eating it? Doesn't it taste good?* [Kids: No!!!!!!!!!] *What's the problem?* [The kids will say, "It's fake!" or "It's plastic!"]

It's not real, is it? Fruit that's not real might look good on the outside, but it's not sweet. That's because real fruit takes time. [At this point, take out the real fruit from the bag; ask if any want to try this fruit. I took an orange – with skin still on it – and took a huge bite out of it, and communicated my joy at its juiciness and sweetness! An apple would work well, of course.] *I can't make real fruit - only God can make real fruit. The same is true with the fruit of the Spirit – like love, and joy, and peace, and patience, and kindness, and gentleness . . . . You know what our problem is? We often think we can make fruit on our own – apart from God. Only God can make real fruit in us . . . and that fruit will truly be beautiful, and delicious, and will bless and nourish everyone around us who eats of it. We need to ask Jesus to produce real fruit in us. Let's pray . . .*

Prayer

Lord, please create space in us for Your Spirit to work, so we might bear true fruit for You – and Your kingdom, in Your name, Amen.

Fruitful Seeds

Scripture

Matthew 13:31-21
"Another parable He put forth to them saying, 'The kingdom of heaven is like a mustard seed, which a man took and sowed in his field, which is indeed the least of all the seeds; but when it is grown it is greater than the herbs and becomes a tree, so that the birds of the air come and nest in its branches.'"

John 12:24
"Most assuredly, I say to you, unless a grain of wheat falls into the ground and dies, it remains alone; but if it dies, it produces much grain."

1 Corinthians 1:26-28
"For you see your calling, brethren, that not many wise according to the flesh, not many mighty, not many noble are called. But God has chosen the foolish things of the world to put to shame the wise, and God has chosen the weak things of the world to put to shame the things which are mighty; and the base things of the world and the things which are despised God has chosen, and the things which are not, to bring to nothing the things that are. . . ."

Big Idea

God loves to produce great fruit through small and insignificant seeds.

Materials

Large, red apple, and a small knife.

Overview

This is another children's sermon that highlights the "upside down" nature of the gospel – i.e. how God loves to take that which is small, and seemingly insignificant, and lowly, to produce great fruit unto Himself from our meager offering. It is deeply encouraging (i.e. this "builds courage into us") to realize that God can produce such great fruit from our small offerings, for with God, "all things are possible."

Sermon

I've got a piece of fruit here – what kind of fruit is this? [Apple.] *Doesn't this apple look beautiful? Desirable? It's big, and red – it's a pretty significant piece of fruit, isn't it? Now I have a question: This apple has some seeds in it, doesn't it? How many seeds do you think are in this apple?* [At this point the kids will shout out answers. After hearing their response, take out a small knife and cut the apple in half, and count the seeds and remove one of them. Hold it out on your fingertip for the children to see.] *That's a very small seed, isn't it? Not very significant. Now, here's my question: "How many apples do you think are inside this seed?"* [Most of the children will shout out "one or two," but a few will "get it" and give higher numbers – knowing that the seed will produce a tree. One of the kids gave this answer: "More than twenty-five, but less than a hundred." I responded, "I think you are going to be a mathematician someday!"] *It's amazing isn't it? This one small seed can produce a tree, which can produce hundreds, maybe thousands of apples! That's pretty cool, isn't it? That reminds me of how God loves to take small, insignificant things, and produce great fruit through them. Isn't that encouraging? Let's pray . . .*

Prayer

Lord, thank You that You love to produce great fruit through small insignificant things like us. Amen.

Gimbals and Orientation

Scripture

Matthew 16:25
"For whoever desires to save his life will lose it;
but whoever loses his life for My sake will find it."

John 17:16
"They are not of the world,
just as I am not of the world."

Big Idea

We become a steady point of reference for those who are swayed by the pulls of the world when we keep a loose grip on the ways and things of this world.

Materials

Candleholder with gimbals (i.e. a candle holder whose base pivots). These can be hard to find; the best place to find one is in "nautical" type stores along the coast that have sailing/ship antiques; or possibly stores that sell various kinds of candle holders. You will also need a candle and matches.

Overview

I was at the ordination ceremony of a friend when I first became intrigued by gimbals. A man (who was a mentor of sorts to my friend) shared some words of encouragement and used gimbals to illustrate his message. Gimbals are essential in modern day space flight, as they provide orientation and a point of reference for the spacecraft. But the ancient predecessors to these modern gimbals could be found on old sailing ships. Very simply, it is a candle attached to a base – which is on a moving, rotating axis. If the ship would lean severely to the right or left, the base of the candleholder would rotate with the ship, the candle itself would remain vertical. Therefore, though a ship be tossed about by the waves on the sea, the candle would always remain upright – pointing the way up – and giving all who would see it a sense of orientation. However, gimbals only work if the candleholder is loosely connected to the base. If it is tightly attached, the candle would sway along with the base – becoming one with the ship's move-ment. It is crucial for the candleholder to be "loosely attached" to the base in order for it to remain oriented in the vertical. So it is with our lives in this world: if we become tightly attached, we become oriented to the circumstances and ways of the world around us. But if we keep a loose grip, we are able to point the way to God – being free from the pulls and leanings of the world around us.

Sermon

Hi everyone! Does anybody know what this is? [Hold up the candle-holder with gimbals. Light the candle with a match.] *Most of the kids shouted out, "Candle!" To which I responded, "Yes – but it's a very special kind of candleholder."* I then proceeded to show them how if the base swayed to the right or left, the candle would remain upright. *"Isn't this cool? Does anyone know what this special kind of candle holder is called?"* [Note: None of the kids knew what it was called. I even asked the adults if they knew, and not one adult in all three services knew what it was called!] *"A modern day version of this is found on the space shuttle; but hundreds of years ago these could be found on ships. If you put it on the table so you could have light to eat by, look what happens if the ship started to sway . . . no matter how much the ship was tossed by the waves, the candle would always remain upright! Now the key to this working right is that the candleholder needs to be loosely attached to the base – which allows the candle to remain pointed upwards even if the base was tilted. But if it is secured too tightly, then the candle will move the same way as the base – and the candle will become disoriented just like the rest of the ship. This reminds me of our lives here in this world. If we become overly attached to what happens to us in this world, and the things of this world, we'll lose our way and become disoriented along with everyone else. But God wants us to "loosen our grip" – and to not hang on so tightly to this world. That way, we can be the ones who remain upright and can point others to God – when everything around us is disoriented."*

Prayer

Lord, help us to be lights that point to You in a dark world. Help us to not hang on to the ways and the things of this world that we might remain oriented toward You – and therefore point others to You. Amen.

God on the Cell Phone

Scripture

Psalm 121:1-4
"I will lift up my eyes to the hills – from whence comes my help? My help comes from the Lord, who made heaven and earth. He will not allow your foot to be moved; He who keeps you will not slumber. Behold, He who keeps Israel shall neither slumber nor sleep."

Matthew 6:6
"But you, when you pray, go into your room, and when you have shut your door, pray to your Father who is in the secret place; and your Father who sees in secret will reward you openly."

1 Kings 18:27
"And so it was, at noon, that Elijah mocked them and said, 'Cry aloud, for he is a god; either he is meditating, or he is busy, or he is on a journey, or perhaps he is sleeping and must be awakened.'"

Big Idea
God always has His ear toward us.

Materials
Cell Phone. [You will need to utilize a good microphone for this; and you will need access to a voice mail or message recorder with which to record a message, which you will call.]

Overview

It's such a simple truth – that God is always there to hear our prayers; yet I have found it often takes monumental faith to believe and engage this truth. Faithlessness in God's omnipresence lies behind a lot of our sin; for if we really believed that the Father hears everything we say and sees everything we do – in the secret place – we might be dissuaded from our sin (or maybe not?). And when our prayers seem to bounce off the ceiling and God seems to hide His face from us in our seasons of wilderness, will we engage in ruthless trust and faithfulness – just to please Him – when there seems to be nothing in it for us? That we have an "Abba, Father" who longs to hear the voice of His children is one of the great scandals of the gospel, says Brennan Manning. His ear is bent toward us – and He is listening.

Sermon

"Do you ever talk with God? Would you like to talk with Him right now? How can we do this? How can we talk with God? [The children will probably give an answer like "prayer."] *How do you talk with God? Simple: Cell phone!* [Pull out a cell phone from your pocket.] *Let's call Him. . . ."*

At this point, call a number – e.g. your voice mail, or message recorder, where you have set up the following message – with a "God-like" voice! Make sure you put the hearing part of the cell phone up to your microphone so that everyone will hear the phone ringing, and will hear this message: *"Hello . . . this . . . is GOD."* (Allow for a five second pause between "God" and the next sentence, as the congregation will probably be laughing for a few seconds.) *"I can't come to the phone right now because I am very busy. But please leave your name and number, and I will get back to you as soon as I can. And remember . . . please wait for the beep."*

As we were all listening to the message from "God," I had a look of astonishment on my face – with my jaw dropped. But the best part was to see the look on the faces of the children, whose astonishment was even greater! *"Now let me ask you: Do you think that was really God?* [No!] *Why not?* [Listen to their answers: Because He said He couldn't talk to you because He was busy!] *Is God ever too busy to listen to us? No! God would never be too busy to talk with us or go to sleep on us. He is always there to listen to our hearts and be with us. Not only that, He LOVES to be with us! How does that make you feel? Let's pray . . .*

Prayer

Jesus, thank You that You are always there, willing and eager to hear our voice, and that You long to be with us. Help us to have faith that You are always there, even when we don't feel it. Amen.

Good For Nothing Worship

Scripture

Matthew 26:6-13

"And when Jesus was in Bethany at the house of Simon the leper, a woman came to Him having an alabaster flask of very costly fragrant oil, and she poured it on His head as He sat at the table. But when His disciples saw it, they were indignant, saying, 'Why this waste? For this fragrant oil might have been sold for much and given to the poor.' But when Jesus was aware of it, He said to them, 'Why do you trouble the woman? For she has done a good work for Me. For you have the poor with you always, but Me you do not have always. For in pouring this fragrant oil on my body, she did it for My burial. Assuredly, I say to you, wherever this gospel is preached in the whole world, what this woman has done will also be told as a memorial to her.'"

Big Idea

Worshipping God may not be the most practical or pragmatic thing we do – but it's what can stir our hearts – and what our hearts long for the most (i.e. God is not so much interested in what we can do for Him, but what we do with Him and in Him.)

Materials

Large peg-board with some hooks and brackets, duct tape, cell phone, keys; and a really nice large piece of art (e.g. of Jesus on the cross, if possible).

Overview

The story of the woman who poured out the costly oil on Jesus strikes at our "religious sensibilities." Jesus seems to make it a point of shattering our belief that we know what's best for the world and what's right in the grand scheme of things (cf. the story of the employer who paid the same wages to the man hired at the last hour as the man who worked all day . . . this irks us.) Often this is true in our approach to worship (and the arts). Why spend time in worship and intimacy with Christ when we could be out there developing programs and feeding the hungry and saving the world? Why "endow the arts" when we could be building needed roads? It's not that such things aren't important or needed, but Jesus is always concerned that we not neglect our primary need – the deepest need of the heart. Art has the ability to stir the heart and inspire the imagination – which in turn will lead to a real fruitfulness – the kind that comes from abiding in the vine.

Sermon

"Good morning!" I said, "Hey – I need your help with something. I am in the process of redecorating my office, and I'm just about done. But there's this one large wall that's got nothing on it; and I'm trying to decide what to put up on this wall. I've narrowed it down to two possibilities – let me show you." [At this point, bring out the large peg board.] "I could put this nice peg board up on the wall. Don't you think this is cool? Look how useful it is! [At this point put several hooks in the pegboard to hang things.] I can use this to hang my keys, to hang up my hat, a place to rest my cell phone, and even a place to hang my duct tape! It sure is useful, isn't it? Well, I'm trying to decide between this pegboard, and this. . . . " [At this point, bring out the work of art.] Now, let me ask you, which of these do you think I ought to put up on my wall: The pegboard, or the art? [The majority of the kids said "The art" – and then I challenged them.] "The art? But look how useful the pegboard is. This artwork is not useful, in fact, it's not useful for anything, is it? Or is it?" [At this point, one of the kids yelled out, "But the art is beautiful!"] "Exactly! The pegboard may be useful, but that doesn't mean that it's necessarily more important. Art can inspire our hearts and take our breath away – much more than some old pegboard! I think it would make a great choice for my office, don't you?"

Prayer

Lord, thank You for the beautiful things in life that You give us that inspire our hearts and change us forever. Amen.

Grapes of Wrath

Scripture

2 Corinthians 4:17
"For our light affliction, which is but for a moment, is working for us a far more exceeding and eternal weight of glory. . . ."

Isaiah 53:5
"But He was wounded for our transgressions, He was bruised for our iniquities. . . ."

Big Idea

Sometimes God allows suffering to make something very precious to Him.

Materials

A bunch of grapes (purple - e.g. Concord grapes), bottle of red wine, bottle of grape juice, sheet of plastic, towel, chair. Place everything in a brown paper bag.

Overview

This is one of my favorite children's sermons. The truth it conveys is startling — even sobering; yet is of extreme beauty. Jesus was crushed that we might be healed. And God calls us to carry our own crosses and suffer for Jesus' sake (Phil. 1:29) Few children's sermons convey such joy and solemnity at the same time.

Sermon

Do you know what these are? (Hold up the grapes.) *Don't these look good? They are so beautiful, so tender, and they look so juicy and good, don't they? I bet a lot of tender loving care went into raising these grapes, don't you think? Well, what would you think of me if I . . .* (Here, quickly get out the sheet of plastic and put it on the floor, and then remove your shoes and socks as quickly as you can. The congregation should start catching on and will probably begin to sense what might be coming. Then, put the grapes down on the plastic and begin crushing the grapes with your bare feet!) For humor, take one of the crushed grapes and hold it up and ask one of the kids, *"Want a grape?"* Then ask again, *"So, what do you think of me for crushing these beautiful, tender, juicy grapes?"* (Some will probably say that you're mean.)

Well, let me ask you this: What if we took all this juice here, and we put it into a bottle, and we then let it sit for . . . oh . . . a few months – or a few years. Do you know what you would get? Here, play off their answers. It was at this point that the senior pastor and I did some ad-libbing that provided some fun. One of kids yelled, "Wine!" But I then pulled out the bottle of grape juice from the brown paper bag and said, *"No, you'd get grape juice!"* At this point, the pastor then commented, "That's because we're Presbyterian!" To which I responded, *"That's right! But if we were Episcopalians, we'd get a fine bottle of wine!"* And here I pulled out the bottle of red wine from the paper bag. The adults in the congregation laughed.

Do you see, it seemed pretty mean when I crushed those grapes, but I needed to do that in order to make this bottle of fine wine. In the same way, God sometimes allows us to get crushed – sometimes He allows really bad things and hard things to happen to us, doesn't He? He doesn't do it to be mean to us, but oftentimes He does it to produce something really precious to Him. It's kind of like what He did to Jesus – remember? When God allowed Jesus to suffer on the cross, a really beautiful thing came out of it, didn't it? From that came our forgiveness!

*Note: When the children are dismissed, there's obviously going to be quite a mess on the stage! I asked one of the other pastors to help me by folding the plastic sheet so that all the crushed grapes and juice were safely inside; and then put it in a trash bag. While he' was doing this, I sat in the chair and wiped my feet with a towel.

Prayer

Lord Jesus, thank You that You were crushed for our sins. And thank You that, when You sometimes allow us to be crushed, we can remember Jesus, and know that You will make something beautiful out of our lives when we are crushed. Amen.

Human Yellow Highlighters

Scripture

James 1:19
"So then, my beloved brethren, let every man be swift to hear, slow to speak. . . ."

Hebrews 10:24
"And let us consider one another in order to stir up love and good works."

Big Idea

We bring encouragement to others when we actively listen to people's stories, prayerfully looking for evidences and fingerprints of God.

Materials

Yellow highlighter pen, book.

Overview

I've long believed that one of the greatest gifts we can offer others is our curiosity and intrigue. People are longing to have someone listen (actively listen) to their stories. Many don't have anyone to do this, so they pay someone to do it. Community is intended to provide a safe place for people to tell their stories, so that others might help "interpret" facets of their story – especially helping them see the fingerprints or evidences of God when they can't see (or believe) them, themselves. In that way, we are like human yellow highlighter pens – highlighting the presence of God even (and especially) in the darkest of stories (indeed – this is where God is usually found.)

Sermon

[Begin by showing the children a yellow highlighter pen.] *Does anyone know what this is? Yes – it's a yellow highlighter. What's it for? You use it to mark and highlight important parts of a book or a story.* [Take out book and mark it with the pen.] *This reminds me of us. . . . I think we are like yellow highlighter pens. And I think we really need each other to be like yellow highlighter pens for one another. Do you know how? Ever have a friend who's discouraged? Or feeling sad? Or feeling like nobody loves them or cares about them? Sometimes, one of the best things we can do is to listen to our friends when they're discouraged, and then point out where we see God at work when they tell their story . . . or show them and remind them where we see that God has indeed loved them or provided for them. Maybe they need to see and hear how much we love them, or their parents love them, or their other friends love them.*

Prayer

Lord, help us to consider one another and listen to one another, and help us to see YOU in each other's stories, so that we might be encouraged, and so that we might stir up love and good deeds. In Your name, Amen.

Hummingbirds and Rainbows
(Thankfulness)

Scripture

Luke 2:9-11
"And behold, an angel of the Lord stood before them, and the glory of the Lord shone around them, and they were greatly afraid. Then the angel said to them, 'Do not be afraid, for behold, I bring you good tidings of great joy which will be to all people. For there is born to you this day in the city of David a Savior, who is Christ the Lord.'"

John 1:14
"And the Word became flesh and dwelt among us, and we beheld His glory, the glory as of the only begotten of the Father, full of grace and truth."

Ephesians 2:1
"And you He made alive, who were dead in trespasses and sins."

Big Idea

Our hearts are filled with gratitude and wonder when the unexpected grace and beauty of God bursts into our lives.

Materials

Photo of a hummingbird and of a rainbow (project on a screen if you have the capability).

Overview

In the book, *Gratitude: the Heart of Prayer*, Brother David Steindl-Rast makes the point that the key to gratitude is the element of surprise – i.e. being surprised by the unexpected "gratuitousness of God" bursting into our lives. It's the stirring in your heart when you encounter an appearance of a hummingbird in your backyard, or a rainbow in the afternoon sky. You drop everything and you must tell somebody. There has been an epiphany – a visitation, and you want everyone to be in on it! We express gratitude and worship when we see and experience the unexpected grace of God in our lives – resurrection power when "we were dead in our trespasses and sins."

Sermon

[Show picture of hummingbird.] *Do you know what this is? (A hummingbird!) Have any of you ever seen a hummingbird in your yard? Think about when you've seen a hummingbird . . . what happens in your heart? Do you get excited? Or do you roll your eyes and say, "Big deal – let's go take a nap." No! You get excited and your heart beats faster and you want to go tell everybody to come and see the hummingbird with you, right? Let me show you another picture.* [Show picture of a rainbow.] *I'm sure you've all seen a rainbow, right? What do you feel inside when you see a rainbow? Do you get bored and sleepy? No! Your heart races and you want to go tell somebody, don't you? Hummingbirds and rainbows are unexpected surprises, aren't they? They're so beautiful, so incredible, that when they come, you drop everything and your heart flutters and you want everyone to experience it with you! That reminds me of what God has done for us: He unexpectedly came and did this beautiful thing – dying on the cross for us. Doesn't that make your heart flutter? Doesn't that make you want to thank Him? Let's pray.*

Prayer

Lord thank You for Your unexpected beauty and grace which bursts into our world – which captivates our hearts and causes us to sing Your praises and give You thanks. Lord, help us to see Your beauty and Your grace this week anew, Amen.

Independence Day

Scripture

John 8:34-36

"Jesus answered them, 'Most assuredly I say to you, whoever commits sin is a slave of sin. And a slave does not abide in the house forever, but a son abides forever. Therefore if the Son makes you free, you shall be free indeed.'"

Romans 8:1-2

"There is therefore now no condemnation to those who are in Christ Jesus, who do not walk according to the flesh, but according to the Spirit. For the law of the Spirit of life in Christ Jesus has made me free from the law of sin and death."

Galatians 5:13-14

"For you, brethren, have been called to liberty; only do not use liberty as an opportunity for the flesh, but through love serve one another. For all the law is fulfilled in one word, even in this: 'You shall love your neighbor as yourself.'"

Big Idea

Jesus frees us from sin so that we might love others in the world.

Materials

US Flag, cross (best if there's a large cross in the church or sanctuary where you are doing this.) [Optional: Photo of your dog for the projection screen.]

Overview

We Americans love and celebrate our independence. Of course in the Scriptures, our *inter-dependence* in the Body of Christ is what is taught and celebrated. But what really marks us as Christians is that we are no longer bound by sin, as a result of the cross — Jesus' atonement gives us freedom from slavery to sin, which frees us to love and lay down our lives for others. We are no longer under law, but under grace. Being independent from *that* is truly worth celebrating!

Sermon

I have a dog – his name is Shiner, and he absolutely freaks out whenever there is thunder. Over the last few nights, we didn't have any thunderstorms, but there have been all these loud explosions. Does anyone know why that is – what's going on? (It's the 4th of July!) *Well, big deal – today's the 1st of July, and next week will be the 8th of July. What's so special about the 4th of July?* (It's Independence Day!) *What does that mean? Independence Day means we're independent from something or someone. Who are we independent from? Actually, Independence Day celebrates how we became independent from Great Britain – so that we were no longer under their control and dominion. What is the symbol of our independence?* (The flag.) [Take out flag and hold up.] *Yes – the flag symbolizes our independence from Great Britain and their control over us.*

[Put flag away. Note: Make sure you fold it properly (lengthwise several times, then triangles) – or you could get some comments. In fact, you might ask if there are any Boy Scouts or Girl Scouts present, as they are taught how to properly fold the flag. When I did this a young boy volunteered to help fold the flag – it was a fun moment.]

Now the Bible says we – all the Christians in the world – not just in this country, but anyone who believes in Jesus, are a "holy nation." Do we have a symbol? What's our symbol as Christians? (Point to a cross.) *Yes – the cross is our symbol – and it's a symbol of our independence from something. Do you know what we're independent from? The cross is the symbol of our independence from sin. It no longer has control and dominion over us! And because we're now free from sin, we are able to fully love God and love others!* [At this point I had all the children stand up and point to the cross in the church.] *Let's celebrate our independence from sin by shouting out the word, "freedom!" together. Ready, on the count of three, let's shout out, "freedom." One, two, three: "FREEDOM!!!"* (Shout it like Mel Gibson did in "Braveheart" ☺) *Let's pray.*

Prayer

Lord Jesus, thank You for freeing us from the control of sin. Thank You that You have truly freed us so that we might love You and love others the way You made us to. In Your name, Amen.

Inhale & Exhale
(Worship)

Scripture

Genesis 2:7
"And the Lord God formed man of the dust of the ground, and breathed into his nostrils the breath of life, and man became a living being."

John 4:23-24
"But the hour is coming, and now is, when the true worshippers will worship the Father in spirit and truth; for the Father is seeking such to worship Him. God is Spirit, and those who worship Him must worship in spirit and truth."

Matthew 4:10
"Then Jesus said to him, "Away with you, Satan! For it is written, 'You shall worship the Lord your God, and Him only shall you serve.'"

Revelation 4:10-11
". . . the twenty-four elders fall down before Him who sits on the throne and worship Him who lives forever and ever, and cast their crowns before the throne, saying, 'You are worthy, O Lord, to receive glory and honor and power; for You created all things, and by Your will they exist and were created.'"

Big Idea

When we worship Jesus we live out of the design for which we were created.

Materials

None needed.

Overview

God created us as finite beings. As such, we are designed to and for worship. It's intrinsic to who we are, as beings made in the image of God. Yet we are prone to worshipping lesser things than the greatest good – who is God. We are prone to wander – and we go after and worship lesser things like money or power or control or "being liked." This is the essence of idolatry – worshipping something or someone other than the greatest good. Worship is our natural response to being made in the image of God and being filled by His breath (cf. Genesis 2:7). It is the exhale to His inhale. And if we fail to exhale, we will choke ourselves and die.

Sermon

You all look sleepy this morning! OK, everybody stand up and we're going to do some breathing exercises. Do you know how to inhale? OK, everybody inhale! (Wait a few seconds.) *Everybody exhale! Everybody inhale!* (Wait a few seconds.) *Everybody exhale! Everybody inhale!* (This time, wait twenty or thirty seconds or more – until the kids start to exhale or cough on their own.) *OK – everybody can now exhale! What happens to us if we inhale but don't exhale?* (Several shouted out, "We'll choke!" or "We'll die!") *Yes! If we inhale, but never exhale, we'll choke ourselves and die. Exhaling kind of reminds me of worship. The Bible says that when God created us, He breathed into us His very breath; He poured His life and His love into us. And we came to life! And He created us to worship Him. And when we worship Him, that's like exhaling. We give Him back all that He's poured into us! When we worship Jesus, we're living out of the very design that God created! Just as He created us to breathe by inhaling and exhaling, so He created us to worship Him – because He has poured His Spirit into us.*

Prayer

Lord, thank You for creating us for Yourself. Show us how wonderful it is to worship You. Help us in our weaknesses, because we're always tempted to worship lesser things – like money or comfort or control or being liked by people. Help us to worship You with our very breath. In Your name, Amen.

Jesus' Christmas List

Scripture

John 4:23
"But the hour is coming, and now is, when the true worshipers will worship the Father in spirit and truth; for the Father is seeking such to worship Him."

Luke 17:15-18
"And one of them, when he saw that he was healed, returned, and with a loud voice glorified God, and fell down on his face at His feet, giving Him thanks. And he was a Samaritan. So Jesus answered and said, 'Were there not ten cleansed? But where are the nine? Were there not any found who returned to give glory to God except this foreigner?'"

Big Idea

God's greatest desire is for worshippers.

Materials

Sign, or overhead, or projection, etc. which will simply have a number with an exclamation point – the number will be the number of days until Christmas (e.g. 130!)

Overview

We hear it all the time, and many times it is us (the pastors) who indulge in the sentiment: "That was great worship!" or, "The worship was flat this morning," or, "Let's *do* some worship." It has become all too common in the church to refer to worship as something out there, or something *outside of us* – something that we critique. Yet worship is not music – thought music is a part of it. And worship is not deeds – though they can be offered as an act of worship. Worship has to do with the *posture of the heart*. And this truth lies at the heart of free will (and thus necessitates the very possibility of evil and the freedom to reject God). God can never force us to worship: yet all that He is and all that He has done is geared toward His desire and longing for that very thing. He longs for worshippers – those who respond to Him by choice, allured by His great acts of love and sacrifice on their behalf. I once heard it said that the greatest gift we can offer God is *faith* – faith that believes in God's love and goodness *when everything around us seems to indicate otherwise*. That is worship. And the Father longs for it.

Sermon

I had our A/V man project the number "130!" up on our large screens as the children were coming up. I could tell that many of them saw it and were looking up at it as they came forward. *"Why are you all looking up there? Oh! There's a number up there – the number 130! What could this mean? Does anyone have any idea what significance the number 130 has today?"* Let them guess; if they have trouble, give them the following hint. *"Let me give you a hint: the number stands for days – and today it's the number 130!"* *"There are only 130 more days until Christmas! Now, are any of you making a list of what you'd like for Christmas? Do any of you ever do that – make a list of what you'd like for Christmas?"* When I said this, it was interesting that very few of the kids raised their hands or indicated in the affirmative. I then remarked (semi-jokingly – but with some sense of seriousness) *"Now, I'm not sure as to whether keeping a list of what we want for Christmas is a good thing or not, but let me ask you this: Do you think Jesus has a list of what He would like for Christmas?"* Interestingly, almost all the kids raised their hands! *"Christmas is Jesus' birthday – what do you think He wants for Christmas? What do you think is on His list?"* At two of our three services, a child yelled out, "Us!" *"Yes! I think what Jesus wants most for Christmas are worshippers. And that's why we come and gather here at church, isn't it? To worship Jesus! So do you think Jesus is happy right now? Yes – I think He's very happy. And I think we have the opportunity every Sunday, and whenever we worship Jesus, to give Him an early Christmas present!"*

Prayer

Lord, we know that Your great desire is for people who would worship You. Open our eyes that we might see Your presence and Your goodness and Your love. For when we are able to see that, we will worship You with all our heart. And that will make You happy. And that is our desire, Jesus – to please You. We love You, Jesus. Amen.

Labor Day
The Greatest Labor of Love

Scripture

Exodus 20:8-10
"Remember the Sabbath day, to keep it holy. Six days you shall labor and do all your work, but the seventh day is the Sabbath of the Lord your God. In it you shall do no work."

Isaiah 53:11
"He shall see the labor of His soul, and be satisfied."

Hebrews 4:9-11
"There remains therefore a rest for the people of God. For he who has entered His rest has himself also ceased from his works, as God did from His. Let us therefore be diligent to enter that rest."

John 6:27-29
"Do not labor for the food which perishes, but for the food which endures to everlasting life, which the Son of Man will give you, because God the Father has set His seal on Him. Then they said to Him, 'What shall we do, that we may work the works of God?' Jesus answered and said unto them, 'This is the work of God, that you believe in Him whom He sent.'"

Phil. 1:21-22
"For to me to live is Christ, to die is gain. But if I live on in the flesh, this will mean fruit from my labor."

Materials

None needed. (If you have a large cross in your church, this may be utilized.)

Big Idea

Nothing beautiful came into being without great labor and sacrifice. (The most beautiful thing on earth — God's church — came into being through the greatest labor of love.)

Overview

Labor Day is a day when we cease from our work to celebrate its value and role in our lives. It is a day to "stop" and to "rest" – and to celebrate the results of our labor. It is very similar to the idea of "Sabbath." For on the Sabbath day we rest from our work to celebrate a bigger, more defining work that set us free to be the people of God. Most of us fall into the belief that we work to "make money." We may indeed earn wages for our money, but this is far too small a purpose for our work. The purpose of work is to be fruitful – to produce something of value and beauty that reflects our Creator – in whose image we are made. To work is to live out the *imago dei* (image of God) – the very reason we were created.

Sermon

Do you know what holiday weekend this is? (Labor Day!) *Yes – but now let me ask you this: What is "labor?" What does "labor" mean?* (One child yelled out, "God!" – to which I quickly responded, "On most Sundays that answer would work . . . but not today" – which brought a lot of laughter from the adults.) *Does anyone know what labor is? How about you moms out there . . . do you know what labor means?* (Most of the moms nodded their heads.) *Labor means work! Now, let me ask you this: "Why do we work? What is the purpose of labor?"* (Many children yelled out, "To make money!") *Well, money is a part of it, but that's not the real reason we work. The real purpose of work is to be fruitful . . . to make something beautiful. Anything beautiful we see in the world is here because somebody labored and worked to bring it into existence. You are all here because your mother labored . . . and your mom and dad continue to labor by feeding you and dressing you and parenting you. And look at this church building . . . isn't it beautiful? This beautiful building wouldn't be here if it weren't for hundreds of workers who labored to build it. But remember, this is the church <u>building</u> . . . but it's not the church. The building contains the church. So who is the church? US!!!! We are the church – all of us who gather in this building. Now let me ask you: Who sacrificed and labored to make the church?* (At this point I ran over to the large cross we have in our church and I climbed up on it and embraced it.) *Who labored to make the church? JESUS!!! Yes – and it was the greatest labor of love ever* *done . . . He bled and sacrificed and died so that we could live and come together and be His church! You know, in this country, we celebrate our labor once a year on Labor Day. But we get to celebrate Jesus' labor every week – it's what we call the Sabbath; where we come together once a week from our work and we rest and we celebrate the work of God on our behalf.*

Prayer

Lord, thank You for Your labor of love on our behalf. Thank You for dying on the cross for us. Help us to enter into that rest that You provide for us by Your great work. In Your name, Amen.

Left Behind

Scripture

Philippians 1:20b-24

"Christ will be magnified in my body, whether by life or by death. For to me to live is Christ, to die is gain. But if I live on in the flesh, this will mean fruit from my labor; yet what I shall choose I cannot tell. For I am hard pressed between the two, having a desire to depart and be with Christ, which is far better. Nevertheless, to remain in the flesh is more needful for you."

2 Corinthians 5:1-7

"For we know that if our earthly house, this tent, is destroyed, we have a building from God, a house not made with hands, eternal in the heavens. For in this we groan, earnestly desiring to be clothed with our habitation which is from heaven, if indeed, having been clothed, we shall not be found naked. For we who are in this tent groan, being burdened, not because we want to be unclothed, but further clothed, that mortality may be swallowed up by life. Now He who has prepared us for this very thing is God, who also has given us the Spirit as a guarantee. So we are always confident, knowing that while we are home in the body we are absent from the Lord. For we walk by faith, not by sight."

Big Idea

To live is Christ, to die is gain.

Materials

Sound system which can play the sound of a helicopter.

Overview

Much of our Christian culture is taken up with the idea of the "rapture" – of escaping the suffering of this present world, leaving behind unbelievers who will experience tribulation. Now of course there is a lot of debate on matters of eschatology and the end times, but I am concerned about a way of thinking which might convey to the world a self-serving and narcissistic mindset – that God would come and rescue His chosen while "leaving behind" a dying world to suffer. The Scriptures here and much of the New Testament (including Revelation) seem to me to portray a different kind of God – one who calls and chooses His people *in order to go into and rescue a suffering, dying world –* rather to be kept safe from such suffering. But however it falls out in the end, Paul makes clear that whether we live or die, it is win-win! To depart and be with Christ is better, but to remain is more needed.

Sermon

Imagine you were on an island, and a bunch of you were there fighting a war – a war between good and evil; and there was a lot of fighting and death and pain and suffering . . . but the cool thing was that Jesus Himself came and joined you – and everyone was encouraged because Jesus was with you as you fought this battle. But then, one day, you heard this!! [Sound of helicopter.]

Wow! Check this out! In the midst of the battle, all of the sudden this huge helicopter appears from heaven . . . and the pilot of the helicopter lands on the battlefield and offers you the choice: You can come with him and he'll fly you away and take you to heaven; or you can be left behind with Jesus, to continue to fight the battle between Good and Evil with Him and with all your friends and those you love.

Which would you choose? To board the helicopter for heaven? Or be left behind with Jesus? [Let them answer; you'll probably get mixed responses.]

That's a tough question, isn't it? The apostle Paul had a hard time with this question. In the book of Philippians he wrote that he was torn apart by this question: For he knew that to depart this world and be with Christ in heaven was really cool! – yet to be left behind here was much more needed. And Paul said that, "To live is Christ – to die is gain." In reality, it's God who chooses when we go to heaven. But the really, really cool thing is, as long as we're left behind here, Christ is in us and He is with us! Let's pray . . .

Prayer

Lord Jesus, give us vision and courage to see the suffering of those around us, and to love them and help them. Thank You that You care for us and will take care of us, and that we can trust You with our lives. Amen.

Let's Build a Chicken

Scripture

1 Corinthians 12:14-20
"For in fact the body is not one member but many. If the foot should say, 'Because I am not a hand, I am not of the body,' is it therefore not of the body? And if the ear should say, 'Because I am not an eye, I am not of the body,' is it therefore not of the body? If the whole body were an eye, where would be the hearing? If the whole were hearing, where would be the smelling? But now God has set the members, each one of them, in the body just as He pleased. And if they were all one member, where would the body be? But now indeed there are many members, yet one body."

Galatians 1:15-16a
"But when it pleased God, who separated me from my mother's womb and called me through His grace, to reveal His Son in me, that I might preach Him among the Gentiles. . . ."

Big Idea

God loves and needs all of our unique and special body parts in order to make a perfect body.

Materials

Package of raw chicken legs (you'll need at around six legs), tooth-picks, plate, napkins, bag, clean-wipes (to clean your hands after!)

Overview

In the book of Galatians, Paul proclaims the essence of calling: "But God, who separated me in my mother's womb, and *called me through His grace, to reveal His Son in me*, that I might preach Him among the Gentiles . . ." The essence of the New Covenant concept of calling lies in this truth – that Jesus reveals Himself to the entire world through each one of us, uniquely. We uniquely reflect some facet of Jesus in a way that nobody else can and does. And He does this through the operation of His grace at work in our lives – in our very weaknesses, wounded-ness, and wickedness. James Houston once observed, "Your Achilles' heel will be the threshold of God's grace to you." It is where we are weak, and wounded, and struggle, that we will need God (see 2 Cor. 4:5-12). It is there that our calling will be forged [Case in point: Simon Barjona – unstable, impetuous; boldly proclaiming his allegiance one minute, and denying he ever knew Jesus the next. Yes Jesus has a vision for him: He shall be "Peter" – the Rock, the point of stability upon which He would build His church.] We so need to embrace our truest identity, which will be formed out of our unique story. We need to ask ourselves, "How is Christ being uniquely revealed in me – through His grace at work in my life?" When we get ahold of this, we will never wish to be somebody else, or be "like" somebody else again. And we will begin to embrace our unique calling.

Sermon

"This morning I have something fun we're going to do together. Do you know what we're going to do? We're going to build a chicken! Can you help me? OK, if we are going to build a chicken, what do we need?" From this point on, let the kids shout out different body parts – e.g. legs, wings, head, beak, etc. As they shout out a body part, take out a chicken leg from the bag of chicken legs. Assemble them together with a toothpick! The more bizarre looking, the better! When you use up all the chicken legs, hold up the chicken to the kids.

"OK! Here's my chicken! What do you think?" At this point, the kids started giggling. *"What's the matter? What's wrong with our chicken?"* One of the children shouted out, "It needs a life!" The whole church burst out in laughter. *"But what's wrong with our chicken?"* Another child yelled out, "It needs to be cooked!" Again much laughter. *"But let's back up a minute – we're talking about the creation of the chicken –*

before it's cooked!" Again, laughter. *"What's wrong with our chicken?"* Another child shouted out, "It needs a heart!" At this point, the congregation was just about rolling with laughter, and I played on it with some comments that were basically directed at the adults: *"Gee – we've taught these kids too well! They're all thinking metaphorically! OK guys, lets get a little more basic here – think literally for a minute! Take a close look at this chicken . . . what's wrong with it?"* At this point, there was silence – they seemed baffled. I then screamed out: *"Look at this chicken! THIS CHICKEN IS BIZARRE!"* Then the congregation (and I) just about lost it. Finally, one of the kids shouted out, "It's made of all legs!" I exclaimed, *"YES! The chicken is made of all one body part – chicken legs! And that's one weird chicken now, isn't it?! What this chicken really needs is different body parts, doesn't it?*

"You know, the Bible says that we, the church, are the body of Christ. And we're all made up of very different parts, aren't we? Now what would we be like if all of us were the same – and we all looked alike, and acted alike, and we all had the same gifts? We'd be pretty bizarre, wouldn't we? I think we should be thankful that all of us are different, unique, and special! Don't you? If all the church were one body part – like a foot, that would make us pretty weird, wouldn't it? Or if we were all . . . noses . . . now that would be REALLY scary, wouldn't it?" [I was playing on the fact that I have a very large nose – the kids and the congregation all laughed.] *"Let's thank Him that we're all different and unique . . ."*

Prayer

Dear God, thank You for making each of us unique, each of us with different gifts – all to build up the body of Christ. Forgive us for envying others and trying to be like others, or wishing we were like someone else. Lord, help us see the unique ways You are displaying Yourself in each one of us. Amen.

Light in Darkness

Scripture

John 1:4-5
"In Him was life, and the life was the light of men. And the light shines in the darkness, and the darkness did not comprehend it." (Note: the NKJV points out that the Greek word for "comprehend" can be translated, "overcome."

Ephesians 5:13-14
"But all things that are exposed are made manifest by the light, for whatever makes manifest is light. Therefore He says, 'Awake you who sleep, arise from the dead, and Christ will give you light."

Ephesians 4:7-10
"But to each one of us grace was given according to the measure of Christ's gift. Therefore He says: 'When He ascended on high, He led captivity captive, and gave gifts to men.' Now this, 'He ascended' – what does it mean but that He first descended into the lower parts of the earth? He who descended is also the One who ascended far above all the heavens, that He might fill all things."

1 Timothy 1:15
"This is a faithful saying and worthy of all acceptance, that Christ Jesus came into the world to save sinners, of whom I am chief."

Big Idea

The darker it gets, the brighter Jesus shines.

Materials

Candle, matches, flashlight. If your church/meeting room has spotlights, utilizing these will also be a plus.

Overview

The statement nearly floored me, and it's something I'll never forget: "If you *really* want to see Jesus, go to hell." Peter, our pastor, was preaching on the descent of Jesus: Of His descent into this fallen world in His incarnation, and of His descent into hell through His crucifixion. Jesus comes to the dark places – the broken places, our own self-inflicted "hells" – so that He might shine His light in these dark places, and liberate us from the bondage of the darkness into the glory of His light. Sadly, I have observed among Christians and churches that much of our energy is spent trying to keep hell from invading our gates, our "sanctuary." Yet Jesus did not say that the *gates of the church would prevail against the onslaught of hell*, but He said that the *gates of hell would not prevail against the onslaught of the church* (Matthew 16:18)! Jesus brings His light into the dark places of our world – and of our hearts. And the amazing thing, as this children's sermon shows, is that the darker the world or our heart is, the brighter the light of Jesus can and will shine! This provides great encouragement and hope to sinners. And it will hopefully free us from living our lives in this world in fear or on the defensive. We can go into the dark places. We need not fear. For the greater the darkness, the stronger the light!

Sermon

[Begin by lighting a candle and showing it to the children.] *Can everyone see this candle?* (They all said that they could.) *But what about you way in the back of the church – can you see this candle? Hey Larry.* (Larry was our media guy in the A/V booth when I did this.) *Can you please turn up the lights on my candle?* (At this, Larry turned up the spotlight on me and on the candle.) *Does that help? Can you now see the light any better?* (The children shouted out, "No!") *Well, maybe if I shine my flashlight on the candle we'll be able to see it better.* (At this I took out a flashlight and attempted to shine it on the flame of the candle). *Does that help? Can you see it better now?* (The children shouted out, "No!") *You know, maybe I've got it wrong. Hey Larry, let's try turning <u>down</u> the lights.* (At this, Larry turned down not only the spotlights, but also all the house lights. The candle grew incredibly bright.) *Does that help? Can you see the light now?* ("Yes!") *Isn't that interesting: the darker it is, the brighter this light shines! You know the Bible says that Jesus is the* *"light of the world." Now I find that a comforting thought – that no matter how dark things get in our world, or in my heart, the darker things get, the brighter the light of Jesus can shine. Isn't that cool? It helps me relax – and not be in fear! Let's pray.*

Prayer

Lord, thank You for the light that shines in the darkness; because the darkness has not and cannot and will not overcome it. Thank You for shining Your light into our darkest places. Thank You that we don't have to be afraid of the dark places in our lives and in our world. Amen.

Living by the Sword

Scripture

Matthew 26: 51-52
"And suddenly, one of those who were with Jesus stretched out his hand and drew his sword, struck the servant of the high priest, and cut off his ear. But Jesus said to him, 'Put your sword in its place, for all who take the sword will perish by the sword.'"

John 18:10-11
"Then Simon Peter, having a sword, drew it and struck the high priest's servant, and cut off his right ear. The servant's name was Malchus. So Jesus said to Peter, 'Put your sword into the sheath. Shall I not drink the cup which my Father has given Me?'"

Ephesians 6:17
"And take the helmet of salvation, and the sword of the Spirit, which is the Word of God."

Hebrews 4:12
"For the Word of God is living and powerful, and sharper than any two-edged sword, piercing even to the division of soul and spirit, and of joints and marrow, and is a discerner of the thoughts and intents of the heart."

Big Idea

A sword can change a person's mind, but only love can change the heart.

Materials

Sword, sheath. (It helps to have a real, solid sword. Most of the kids – and adults – were enthralled by the sword I used.)
[Please Note: Obviously, swords are quite dangerous. For this sermon I went up on the stage at a distance from the kids (normally I'm on floor level with them) so I could eliminate the risk of an accident, and to put the kids (and their parents!) at ease.]

Overview

Jesus said, "All who take the sword will perish by the sword." Clearly, the kind of sword you wield will determine the kind of life – and death – you will have. So often we're tempted to fight with "weapons" that are familiar and easy for us to run to – weapons like revenge, retaliation, and self-protection . . . an "eye for an eye" approach to life. Yet Jesus resists this way. As our pastor Peter so poignantly observed (with regard to the story of Peter and Malchus), "It's hard to get people to listen when you're cutting off their ears." It's hard to love our enemies when we're shouting at them and condemning them. On the other hand, wielding the "Sword of the Spirit" – which is the Word of God – may lead to your own death (death to your "self"). The apostle Peter had a history of wielding his own sword instead of that of the Spirit – forbidding Jesus to go to Jerusalem to die, even though such a death would lead to his own life. Yet the Sword of the Spirit – the Word of God – will always produce life, for the Word of God *is* The Life Himself – Jesus.

Sermon

Check out this sword! Pretty cool, huh? [I took the sword out of its sheath.] *Let me ask you a question: "What can this sword do?"* The children yelled out answers such as "It can stab things," and "It can kill things." *Yes, a sword can do that. Can a sword protect you?* [Yes!] *Can a sword hurt people?* [Yes!] *Can a sword start a war?* [Yes!] *Can a sword end a war?* [Yes!] *Can a sword cut off someone's ear?* [Yes!] *Yes, it can. But the problem is, if you cut off someone's ear they might not be able to hear anything you want to say to them. Does anyone remember the story in the Bible when somebody's ear got cut off by a sword?* [A few of the kids nodded their heads.] *It's when the soldiers came to arrest Jesus when He was in the Garden of Gethsemane. Do you remember what Peter did when the soldiers tried to get Jesus? He drew his sword and cut off the high priest's servant's ear. The servant's name was Malchus. But do you remember what Jesus did next? He picked up the ear and he put it back on the servant and healed him! And do you remember what He said to Peter?* [One child yelled out, "You're a bad boy!"] *Well, He may have said that, but the Bible says He then told Peter to put his sword away. Let me ask you this: Can a sword change someone's mind?* [The kids were a bit mixed in their response to this – some said yes, others shook their heads no.] *I think it can change someone's mind. Imagine if someone was trying to steal my car and then I pulled out my sword and they changed their mind – and ran away! Now let me ask you one final question: Can a sword change someone's heart?* [All the kids shook their heads, "No!"] *No! The only sword that I know of that can change a heart is the Sword of the Spirit. And the Sword of the Spirit is the Word of God! Does anyone know who the Word of God is? Yes – it's Jesus.*

Prayer

Lord, so often our weapons are not Your weapons. And our words are not Your words. Please help us, Lord, to lay down our weapons – weapons like anger and jealousy and unforgiveness and revenge, so that we learn to use Your weapons – the weapons of love and sacrifice – for the sake of others. And help us to use Your words. For You are the Word – living and active, and sharper than any two-edged sword. In Your name, Amen.

Lord of the Dance

Scripture

Matthew 11:16-17
"But to what shall I liken this generation? It is like children sitting in the marketplaces and calling to their companions, and saying, 'We played the flute for you, and you did not dance.'"

Luke 15:25, 28
"Now his older son was in the field. And as he came near and drew near to the house, he heard music and dancing . . . but he was angry and would not go in. Therefore his father came out and pleaded with him."

John 10:30-31
"I and My Father are one."
'Then the Jews took up stones again to stone Him.'"

Big Idea

The Trinity is like three people in a dance; the better they dance together, the harder it is to tell them apart, even though they are three separate persons.

Materials

No materials needed – but you will need the help of the band (worship team, worship leader, etc.) to play some music for you. Prepare them beforehand about this.

Overview

I recall how in seminary we spent an entire class trying to come up with analogies to better understand the mystery of the Trinity. As I recall, every one of the analogies were from the scientific realm – e.g. an "egg" (shell, white, yolk), a triangle, the "triple-point," of water, etc. Yet the one thing that was so obvious was the one thing we neglected entirely: That the Trinity is about a *relationship*. Eugene Peterson and others have observed how the early church Fathers, in trying to somehow understand this mystery, came up with a Greek word: *perichoresis*. The word *"choresis"* means "dance," while *"peri"* means "around." The trinity is best understood as a dance – Father, Son, and Holy Spirit. And in a good dance, like Ginger Rogers and Fred Astaire, the partners move in such unison and with such coordination and fluidity that they almost become a blur; they move as one, while still remaining individuals in the dance. Our God is the Lord of the Dance, and He longs to bring us into His dance – if we would follow His lead.

Sermon

"Okay, who here likes to dance?" Almost everyone raised their hand when I asked this question. (A thought to ponder: Would the percentage have been so high had I asked the adults?) *"I need three volunteers!"* Bring them up on the stage. *"Okay, when the music starts, I want you to all dance together, okay? All right – hit it!"* [Ask the band to play something fast-paced with a catchy beat – like polka music, or even the music from the song, "Lord of the Dance," if they know it.] *"Now dance! Faster! Faster! Dance together! Swing those arms and stomp those* feet! Swing your partner!" When they finished their dance, the congregation (at each of our three services) gave the kids quite an ovation. Now ask the children who were watching: *"When they were dancing really fast, could you tell them apart?"* [At two of the three services, the kids said "Yes!" The congregation laughed, as they knew it was not the answer I was looking for!] I shook my head and waved my arms, and shouted out, *"Okay – but if they were really good dancers, do you think we could tell them apart?"* [No!] *Because if you can dance really well together, you move together so well that you start to move in one motion – and it becomes hard to tell you apart! That's kind of the way it is with God. Because our God is a Trinity, right – Father, Son, and Holy Spirit. Now that's really hard to understand – that we have one God, but there are three persons. But maybe you can think of this idea – that when two or three partners dance really well together, and move together in love, it's like they become one – even though they still are separate persons.*

Prayer

Lord God, thank You that You exist as Father, Son, and Holy Spirit. And thank You that You love to dance – and more than that, that You love to invite us into the dance with You – to dance with You forever – in love. Thanks for inviting us in. Amen.

Loving with Integrity

Scripture

1 John 4:7-8
"Beloved, let us love one another, for love is of God, and everyone who loves is born of God, and knows God. He who does not love does not know God, for God is love."

Romans 7:6
"But now we have been delivered from the law, having died to what we were held by, so that we should serve in the newness of the Spirit and not in the oldness of the letter."

Proverbs 20:5
"Counsel in the heart of man is like deep water; but a man of understanding will draw it out."

Big Idea

How love is conveyed is just as, if not more, important than the words used to convey love.

Materials

None needed.

Overview

Sometimes our words convey one thing when our heart reveals something far different. You can't hide the thoughts and intents of the heart – they will eventually be revealed for all to see. This is why things like fear and anger are never the bottom line; they are merely "symptoms" of something far deeper – matters of the heart. Proverbs says, "Counsel in the heart of man is like deep water; but a man of understanding will draw it out." This children's sermon is very obvious to the children – but is intended to convey a point that, though obvious, often gets lost on us . . . that, like an iceberg, until what lies beneath the "water line" is dealt with, the true intents of our heart will keep rising to the surface. Jesus has given us a new heart, but we sin when we ignore that new heart – where Jesus resides. J. Philip Newell has defined the flesh as "that sinful tendency in us that disregards our inmost self." Where is our focus?

Sermon

[This sermon will necessitate some "pre-service" scouting; you will need to find four or five adults in the service who will feel comfortable being "picked on."] Begin by talking with the children. *Good morning! I've been memorizing a Scripture that I'd like to recite to you . . . it's become very dear and meaningful to me . . . want to hear it?* [Move away from the kids and begin walking down the aisles. Then begin shouting the verse at people you have pre-screened beforehand (in a mean, angry tone) at the top of your lungs: *"BELOVED, LET US LOVE ONE AN-OTHER . . . FOR LOVE IS OF GOD . . . AND EVERYONE THAT LOVETH IS BORN OF GOD AND KNOWETH GOD . . . HE THAT LOVETH NOT . . . KNOWETH NOT GOD FOR GOD IS LOVE . . . BELOVED, LET US LOVE ONE ANOTHER . . . 1 JOHN 4:7-8!"* Then come back to the kids. I take a deep breath, and then talk in a normal, kind voice. *Well, what did you think? Did you like my Bible verse that I memorized?* [Most of the kids will have a look of incredulity on them – there was quite a commotion, and some yelled out, "You were mean!"] *What was the problem? My actions didn't match my words, did they? The "spirit" in which I said the words totally violated the actual words themselves, didn't they? That's why God feels so strongly that it's our hearts that need His touch – we need new hearts, so He can change us from the inside out! Then, good and beautiful words will flow from our hearts in a way that will be lovely to receive by others.*

Prayer

Lord, thank You for giving us a new heart. Help us to live out of that new heart that You have given us. Forgive us for ignoring it some-times, which causes us to fall back into our old ways. Help us to pay attention to Your presence in us, which will then be released from our heart to bless others. Amen.

Lucy's Dying
(Leaning into Suffering)

Scripture

2 Corinthians 1:3-4
"Blessed be the God and Father of our Lord Jesus Christ, the Father of mercies and God of all comfort, who comforts us in all our tribulation, that we may be able to comfort those who are in any trouble, with the comfort with which we ourselves are comforted by God."

Big Idea

We love like Jesus when we engage people in their suffering instead of fleeing or fixing.

Materials

A photo of your elderly dog or cat.

Overview

I came home one day after an especially difficult day at work, and the moment I walked in I could smell the stench. Lucy, our eleven-year-old greyhound, was losing control of her bladder and had been "leaking" all over the house – not only on her "bed," but on the carpet, both upstairs and downstairs. In a moment of frustration, I yelled out (my son was within earshot), "This is getting ridiculous . . . we need to start thinking of putting her down . . . we can't live like this anymore . . . the house stinks!" Later my wife told me how much my tirade had frightened and discouraged my son. I later apologized to him for my outburst, and reflecting on it, I came to see that I was reacting out of the loss of control not so much concerning Lucy's bladder, but my own loss of control – over situations at work, in my life, and Lucy's life. Poor Lucy couldn't help herself, and she was suffering. A flood of conviction came over me as I realized that I had slowly begun to distance myself from Lucy, realizing she was beginning to die. I lay down on the floor next to her, and began to stroke her and kiss her and comfort her – something I hadn't done in weeks. And my heart welled up with compassion and grief.

Sermon

[I began by projecting a photo of our dog Lucy on the screen.] *I want to show you something this morning. Do any of you know what this is? Is it a deer? Is it am aardvark?* [I was playing off the fact that greyhounds are pretty funny looking.] *No – it's a dog! Do you know what kind of dog this is? It's a greyhound – and greyhounds are really fast – and they love to race. In fact, they can run over 40 MPH! But what most people don't realize is that they're mostly couch potatoes – they just hang around the house all day sleeping like lazy dogs. Anyway, this is Lucy – she's our greyhound. But I need to tell you something sad: Lucy is getting very old, and she's become very sick. She has had some seizures, and now she can't control her bladder so she's leaking all over the house. I'm afraid that Lucy is dying. Do any of you have pets? Have any of you had a pet who's died? It's really hard, isn't it? Now, let me ask you, is there anything I can do to help Lucy?* The children then began to yell out suggestions: "You can take her to the vet!" *"Yes, we've taken her to the vet, and he's done everything he can do for her."* "You can give her medicine!" *"Yes, we're giving her lots of medicine right now, and it's helping a little bit, but it can't stop her from dying."* We've done everything we can to help her medically, but again I ask you, is there anything else I can do for her?* At this point, one child cried out, "You can love her!" *Yes! You know what? As Lucy got more and more sick, I realized that I had actually started to pull away from her, because I was afraid that I was going to lose her. But that doesn't help Lucy, does it? What Lucy loves right now more than anything is for me to lay down with her, and to pet her and rub her belly (she loves that!) and to kiss her and stroke her and bring comfort to her.*

I think this is true for anyone in our lives who is suffering. Sometimes we don't know what to do because we can't "fix" their suffering, so we begin pulling away from them. But that's when they need us the most! Does Jesus pull away from us when we suffer? No! The Bible says that He is with us in our sufferings – and He actually gives us the opportunity to be with Him in His sufferings!

Prayer

Lord, please give us the courage to move in and help others when they're suffering – so that we can love them with Your love – so they can be comforted by You through us. In Your name, Amen.

Making Space for Others

Scripture

Genesis 1:1-2
"In the beginning God created the heavens and the earth. And the earth was formless and empty. . . ."

John 14:1-3
"Let not your heart be troubled; you believe in God, believe also in Me. In My Father's house are many mansions; if it were not so, I would have told you. I go to prepare a place for you. And if I go and prepare a place for you, I will come again and receive you to Myself; that where I am, there you may be also."

Philemon 1:21
"But, meanwhile, also prepare a guest room for me, for I trust that through your prayers I shall be granted to you."

Big Idea

Joy in life is when you make space for others.

Materials

None needed.

Overview

Genesis 1:1-2 speaks of the fascinating idea that before there was space and time, there was only God. Therefore, in order for there to be "others" in the universe, God had to sacrifice and "make space" for others – i.e. make room for us to be, to exist. And because God by His very nature and definition is relational in His essence (i.e. the relational nature of the Trinity; the fact that "God is love"), there is great joy for Him when there are others for Him to dialogue with, and engage with. But to be in isolation is antithetical to the very nature of God – and thus there is no joy there.

Sermon

Begin by asking the kids to move back (i.e. you feel crowded in). *"Can you move back . . . some more . . . please? I need space – I need my space – I can't handle this – I need my space! Oh – there's not enough space for me! I think I'll do my children's sermon over there."* [Go far away over to a corner, or empty area in the church, and then begin preaching the sermon to the wall.] *"For today's children's sermon, I want to read Genesis: "In the beginning God created the heavens and the earth; and the earth was empty – and needed filling – and God said . . . God said . . . oh . . . uh . . . this is no fun!"* (Now look back over to the kids.) *"This just doesn't feel right . . . I'm not having any fun . . . there's no joy. What's the problem?* [At this point, some of the kids yelled out, "You're talking to a wall!"] *Yes – I was talking to a wall – and over there, I was alone, wasn't I? And it wasn't much fun. You know, what I've learned is that there's no joy when you don't make space for others in your life. Because if you don't make space for others, you'll be alone – and there's not a lot of joy in your life when you're alone. Does Jesus live alone? No! He's always lived with His Father and the Holy Spirit – and God has great joy in the Trinity – and God shares that joy with us!*

Prayer

Lord, help us to look to You, so that we might be like You – making space for others – so that we might have joy in Your name, Amen.

Memorial Day

Scripture

John 15:12-13
"This is My commandment, that you love one another as I have loved you. Greater love has no one than this, than to lay down one's life for his friends."

Mark 10:45
"For even the Son of Man did not come to be served, but to serve, and give His life a ransom for many."

1 John 3:16-18
"By this we know love, because He laid down His life for us. And we also ought to lay down our lives for the brethren. But whoever has this world's goods, and sees his brother in need, and shuts up his heart from him, how does the love of God abide in him? My little children, let us not love in word or in tongue, but in deed and in truth."

Big Idea

Sacrificing your life for others reveals the greatest love – and points to the greatest lover of all – Jesus.

Materials

Prepare a slide (or Power-Point, or overhead) with the five multiple choice answers to the question "What is Memorial Day?" (See below). It is best if you can scroll down and show the first answer, then add the second, then add the third, and so on.

Overview

As a child I remember my parents taking our family each Memorial Day to visit all the gravesites of our deceased relatives. It was usually an all-day affair. Therefore, my understanding of Memorial Day was that this was a day to honor the dead. Yet that is not the precise meaning of the day. Memorial Day is a day set aside to honor all of those who have given their lives in the armed forces, in order to protect the United States. In laying down their lives, each of them made the ultimate sacrifice – laying down their very lives for the sake of others; for the sake of something greater than themselves. In this these men and women we see played out a saying of Jesus, "Greater love has no man than this, than to lay down one's life for his friends."

Sermon

*Tomorrow is a very important holiday – does anyone know what holiday
it is? [Let them respond.] Yes, tomorrow is Memorial Day. But do you
know the meaning of Memorial Day? Let me ask you (everyone please
look up on the screen) – what is Memorial Day?*
 A. *First day of summer*
 B. *A day of BBQs and parties*
 C. *First day to plant tomatoes with no danger of frost*
 D. *First day you can legally wear white shoes*
 E. *A day to remember and honor men and women in the military who
 died protecting and serving our country.*

*[Note: C & D may elicit laughter from adults.] That's right – E is the cor-
rect answer! Memorial Day is a day when we honor those who gave the
greatest gift – their very life – in order to protect us and serve our country.
That's the greatest kind of love. And who does that kind of love remind
you of? [Jesus!] You got it! Let's pray . . .*

Prayer

Lord God, thank You for the men and women who have gone before
us, who have given the greatest sacrifice – their very own lives – for
the sake of others. Help us to learn from them. Thank You for the way
they reveal Jesus to us – who gave His life so that others could live.
Thank You Jesus for loving us that way. Amen.

Mother's Day Riddle

Scripture

Matthew 12:47-50

"Then one said to Him, 'Look, Your mother and Your brothers are standing outside, seeking to speak with You.' But He answered and said to the one who told him, 'Who is my mother and who are my brothers?' And He stretched out His hand toward His disciples and said, 'Here are My mother and My brothers! For whoever does the will of My Father in heaven is My brother and sister and mother.'"

Hebrews 12:22-23

"But you have come to Mount Zion and to the city of the living God, the heavenly Jerusalem, to an innumerable company of angels, to the general assembly and the church of the first-born who are registered in heaven. . . ."

Big Idea

The church is like our mother, a bride who, having received the love of her groom, births and nourishes her children.

Materials

If your church has video or overhead projection capabilities, it's helpful to project the questions up on the screen so that everyone can see.

Overview

I have always been intrigued by the Roman Catholic concept of viewing the church as our "mother." The more I thought about it, the more the idea of it (and the images associated with motherhood) made sense to me. Many in our churches struggle with their mothers, just as many struggle with the church. They feel disappointed, or let down, or hurt by them. Yet our mothers were there for us and nourished us. Were they perfect? No. Yet God chose them to be the ones through whom He gives us His life.

Sermon

I have a riddle for you today. Are you ready? Tell me if you can figure out who this is. [Ask the questions in a "rapid fire" manner – i.e. don't give them time to give you the answer until you've finished with all the questions. Several of the kids did shout out "Mom" after I asked the questions].

- *Who labors in order to give birth to beautiful children?*
- *Who is always there for her children in time of need?*
- *Who serves an incredible meal every weekend?*
- *Who lovingly disciplines you when you need it?* (One boy shouted out, "Dad" when I asked this question. The entire church broke out with laughter.)
- *Who cleans you when you get dirty and helps you when you're hurt?*

Does anyone know the answer? [Almost all of them shouted out, "Mom!"] Wrong! The correct answer is, "The church!" [I then went back through each question and explained how the church does these things.] So the church is kind of like our mother, isn't it? Well, we all know that today is Mother's Day. So why don't we all stand up, and let's turn around and face the congregation, and let's honor all the moms who are here. Everybody repeat after me:

- *We salute thee*
- *Most awesome progenitors*
- *Of the human species.*
- *Happy Mother's Day!*

[Note: I deliberately try to keep things on the light side with this (hence the silly "repeat after me" sentences), knowing that for some adults in the congregation, this can be a painful day – whether due to struggles with their own mom, or having had a mom who died recently, or being unable to be a mom themselves. I have even had women call me the previous week asking me if the sermon was going to be about mothers that day – for if it was, they would avoid church. When I tell them that we're just doing the children's sermon about it, they are usually OK with that.]

Prayer

Lord, we thank You for our mothers. Thank You for the sacrifices they make in order that we might be born into the world, and to help us grow and live life on this earth. Thank You for Your church, which is like a mother to us. Help us to love each other and do Your will so that all of us would be mothers and brothers and sisters to each other. In Your name, Amen.

Mother's Day Riddle II

Scripture

Luke 13:34
"O Jerusalem, Jerusalem, the one who kills the prophets and stones those who are sent to her! How often I wanted to gather your children together, as a hen gathers her brood under her wings, but you were not willing!"

Genesis 1:2
"The earth was without form, and void; and darkness was on the face of the deep. And the Spirit of God was hovering over the face of the waters. Then God said, 'Let there be light': and there was light."

Galatians 4:26
"But the Jerusalem above is free, which is the mother of us all."

Isaiah 49:15-16
"Can a woman forget her nursing child, and not have compassion on the son of her womb? Surely they may forget, yet I will not forget you. See, I have inscribed you on the palms of My hands; your walls are continually before Me."

Big Idea

A mother's almost supernatural-like abilities reveal the strong and tender care of God for us.

Materials

Rubber or plastic body parts - you can find these at a good costume shop. I used two eyes, an ear, a foot, and a hand. You will need an adult female volunteer whom you will invite up. (Arrange this with them beforehand so they know what to expect.) It's best if you can find a woman who is wearing a long sleeved shirt and pants to attach the body parts to. You will need some large rubber bands and/or clear packing tape, to use to fasten the body parts to the female volunteer.

Overview

While Mother's Day is a wonderful day of celebration for most, for some it is a very painful day. Like the other children's sermon I have for Mother's Day (Mother's Day I), I therefore try to keep things on the light side with this (hence the silly "repeat after me" sentences), knowing that for some adults in the congregation, this can be a painful day – whether due to struggles with their own mom, or having had a mom who died recently, or being unable to be a mom themselves. I have even had women call me the previous week asking me if the sermon was going to be about mothers that day – for if it was, they told me they would avoid church – it's just too painful a topic. When I tell them that we're just doing the children's sermon about it, they are usually OK with that. There are many Scriptures which speak of the tender, motherly aspects of God (some of which are given above) – which speak of God as "hovering" – like a mother hen protecting her chicks. In addition, one of the Hebrew words for God in the Old Testament, "El Shaddai" is usually understood to have the meaning, "The Almighty" or "The Strong One" – for its literal translation is "God of the Mountains." But scholars have pointed out that this can also be literally translated as, "God of the Breasts" – which would convey God's tender, nourishing nature – giving the picture of a child at his mother's breast.

Sermon

I have a riddle for you today. [Note: If possible, it's important that, up to this point in the worship service, there is no mention of this being "Mother's Day" . . . you don't want them to be thinking along those lines, so as not to make the riddle easier to figure out]. *But first, I need a volunteer . . . do I have an adult who can help me? OK – I have a bag with me that contains some body parts. First, I have a couple of eyes – I'm going to attach these to the back of her head* [attach eyes to the back of her head – you can use a rubber band, or some clear tape to do this]. *Now what else do I have here, let's see . . . I have an ear! I'm going to attach this to the side of her head – so now she has three ears!* [Again, use some kind of band or clear tape to do this.] *What else do I have in my little bag here . . . oh – I have an extra hand! I will attach this to her as well* [If she has a sleeve, just tuck it under the sleeve so that the hand sticks out.] *And I think I have one more part – oh yes – I have a foot! Let me put this foot on you!* [Slide the foot up under her pants, so she has an extra foot sticking out of the bottom of her pants.] *OK – now here's my question: What IS this?* [It's fascinating to listen to the children's answers, which ranged from "monster" to "creature" or words like that.] *No . . . that's not what she is . . . doesn't anyone know who this is? It's a MOM!!!* [At this point, there is a loud and startled reaction, and everyone begins to laugh as they start to get the joke, and I begin to elaborate.] *See – everyone knows that moms have an extra ear, and that they can hear everything and know everything you say . . . and of course we all know that moms have eyes on the back of their heads* [this drew the most laughter]; *and we all know that moms seem to have an extra hand for helping, and an extra foot that helps them to be at two or three places at once, right? Moms are pretty incredible, wouldn't you agree? You know, everyone here has a mom. Some of you might have moms who have died, or some of you might have moms whom you have struggles with; but all of us would not be here if it weren't for our moms. Well, we all know that today is Mother's Day. So why don't we all stand up, and let's turn around and face the congregation, and let's honor all the moms that are here. Everybody repeat after me:*

- *We salute thee*
- *Most awesome progenitors*
- *Of the human species.*
- *Happy Mother's Day!*

Prayer

Lord, thank You for our mothers, who birthed us, helped to raise us, and loved us. Help us to honor them today. Thank You that our earthly mothers can reveal the creative, tender, nourishing care that God has for us. Amen.

Mouse Trap

Scripture

1 Corinthians 12:12, 25b-27
"For as the body is one and has many members, but all the members of that body, being many, are one body, so also is Christ. . . . But the members should have the same care for one another. And if one member suffers, all the members suffer with it; or if one member is honored, all the members rejoice with it. Now you are the body of Christ, and members individually."

Big Idea

In the Body of Christ, we are all interconnected, so that when one member suffers, all members suffer.

Materials

None, other than the story of the "Mousetrap" to read. The author of this story is unknown, and it's in the public domain (e.g. see http://www.wow4u.com/mousetrap/index.html.)

Overview

At infant baptisms and dedications, we ask a series of questions to the parents as they stand before the entire congregation. And then we ask the entire congregation a question – that is, if they promise to support this family and love this family as they raise this child. In a large church, a logical issue that emerges for many of the congregation is that they won't have any immediate contact or direct impact on this child or family. Or *will* they? It is here that I like to point out that none of us live our lives in a vacuum. We are all interconnected. And the thoughts we think and the acts we do in secret *do* have an impact on the Body of Christ – so that when I sin in secret, I have an impact on those around me; and when I do righteous acts in secret, this also has an impact on those around me. Some might see this as guilt or fear producing. I see it as just the opposite: knowing that my inner life has an impact not only on me but on the Body of Christ around me, motivates me to live rightly – for the sake of love. The following story illustrates well the connected nature of the Body of Christ.

Sermon

This morning I want to read you a story. Listen closely:

A mouse looked through a crack in the wall to see the farmer and his wife opening a package. What food might it contain? He was aghast to discover that it was a mouse trap. Retreating to the farmyard, the mouse proclaimed the warning: "There's a mouse trap in the house; a mouse trap in the house!"

The chicken in the farmyard clucked and scratched, and raised her head and said, "Excuse me, Mr. Mouse, I can tell this is of grave concern to you, but it is no consequence to me. I cannot be bothered by it."

The mouse turned to the pig and told him, "There is a mouse trap in the house; a mouse trap in the house!" "I am so sorry Mr. Mouse," sympathized the pig, "but there is nothing I can do about it but pray. Be assured you are in my prayers."

The mouse then turned to the cow. "There is a mouse trap in the house; a mouse trap in the house!" But the cow said, "Like . . . wow, Mr. Mouse . . . a mouse trap . . . like I'm in grave danger . . . NOT!" So the mouse returned to the house, head down and dejected, to face the farmer's mouse trap alone.

Now that very night a sound was heard throughout the house, like the sound of a mouse trap catching its prey. The farmer's wife rushed to see what was caught. In the darkness, she did not see that it was a venomous snake whose tail the trap had caught. The snake then bit the farmer's wife. The farmer rushed her to the hospital. She returned home with a fever. Now, everyone knows you treat a fever with fresh chicken soup, so the farmer went out to the farmyard to look for the soup's main ingredient, if you know what I mean! So he fed her some fresh chicken soup.

But his wife's sickness continued, so that friends and neighbors came to sit with her around the clock. To feed them, the farmer had to butcher the pig. But her illness continued, and she was sick for a long time, and more and more people came to visit; so the farmer had the cow slaughtered to provide meat for all of them to eat.

So, the next time you hear that someone is facing a problem and you think that it does not concern you, remember that when there is a mouse trap in the house, the whole farmyard is at risk.

Prayer

Lord, we are all one big family – a part of one body – and when one part is weak or sick, we need to pay attention and care for our brothers and sisters because what affects one of us affects all of us. Help us to see how connected we all are – and love each other as we do ourselves. Amen.

Palm Sunday
The Way of Peace

Scripture

Luke 19:37
"Then, as He was now drawing near the descent of the Mount of Olives, the whole multitude of the disciples began to rejoice and praise God with a loud voice for all the mighty works they had seen, saying: 'Blessed is the King who comes in the name of the Lord! Peace in heaven and glory in the highest.'"

Luke 23:18-21
"And they all cried out at once, saying, 'Away with this Man, and release to us Barabbas' – who had been thrown into prison for a certain rebellion made in the city, and for murder. Pilate, therefore, wishing to release Jesus, again called out to them. But they shouted, saying, 'Crucify Him, crucify Him!'"

Revelation 7:9-10
"After these things I looked, and behold, a great multitude which no one could number, of all nations, tribes, peoples, and tongues, standing before the throne and before the Lamb, clothed with white robes, with palm branches in their hands, and crying out with a loud voice, saying, 'Salvation belongs to our God who sits on the throne, and to the Lamb!'"

Big Idea

We worship when we move from asking what Jesus can do *for* us to asking what Jesus wants *from* us.

Materials

One donkey (be aware you will need to arrange for this months in advance, as the rental of donkeys is a popular thing on Palm Sunday at churches); clothing (to be Jesus) – e.g. robe, sandals, head-dress; palm branches for children.

Overview

This has become a tradition at our church: to have the children form a gauntlet into the church, waving palm branches as Jesus (usually me) rides in on a donkey (our donkey was named "Firecracker".) The whole room is electrified as shouts and songs of Hosanna are offered as Jesus rides in. It signifies the beginning of Holy Week, and the mood is festive. Yet just five days later, these same voices (in the biblical story) who shout out "Hosanna" will be shouting for Jesus' death. What happened? The text gives us a clue, as it says that the multitudes of disciples blessed this King "for all the mighty works they had seen." Perhaps they were anticipating that this earthly king was about to assume His rightful throne and end their oppression under Rome? But five days later, in an act of astonishing humiliation, offering Himself and relinquishing His kingly power, Jesus would be cursed as one deserving of death. The people preferred the *way of Barabbas* – that of human grasping and control. We are continually confronted with these two ways: The *way of Jesus* – submitting ourselves in trust and obedience to the Father's will; or the way of Barabbas – who represents all human effort to bring in the kingdom for ourselves. The *way of peace* versus the *way of violence*. Ironically, "Bar-abbas" literally means, "Son of the Father." Jesus took his place, and shows us what a real "son of Abba" looks like.

Sermon

Dressed as Jesus, I rode into church on the donkey, passing between a gauntlet of children waving palm branches as we all sang "Hosanna." When we got to the front, I dismounted and began to speak to the children. (I spoke with a Middle Eastern accent.) *Hello children! You all know what today is, don't you?* ("Palm Sunday!") *And what did the people do on Palm Sunday?* ("They waved palm branches!") *Yes – they waved palm branches and shouted out "Hosanna" and they worshipped Jesus. However, five days later, on Good Friday, what did these same people do? What did they shout out?* (Several yelled out, "Crucify Him!" They knew the story.) *Yes, can you believe it? This happened only five days later! What happened?* (The children at all three services were dumbfounded when I asked this question.) *Maybe the people were more interested in what Jesus could do for them, instead of what they could do for Jesus. Let me ask you: What does Jesus want from us?* (Several stated, "Love," one said "Worship." And one young boy yelled out, "Our sins!" – which I thought was profound.) *What Jesus wants is us! And He wants us to want Him. That's all. He wants our love and our worship.*

Prayer

[I skipped my usual prayer, not wanting to break from my accent, and simply led the donkey and the children back out of the church while we resumed singing "Hosanna."]

Passion Fruit

Materials

Shopping bag from a familiar health food or grocery store, passion fruit (get passion fruit juice if the fruit is hard to find); printout of Internet article on "passion fruit" (do a search on the Internet for this.)

Overview

The word "passion" has come to mean something akin to desire or strong emotion. It is a striking thing that another term for "Holy Week" or "Easter Week" is *Passion Week*. Mel Gibson's film also thrust this word in the forefront of our imagination. To have passion is to *suffer*. Indeed, it is the ultimate expression of passion: To love someone so passionately that you would be willing to suffer and die for them.

Sermon

[I started by talking with a quiet, boring, monotone voice and a stiff body posture.] *I went to "Wild Oats" today to be "wild."* [Show Wild Oats bag.] *I was talking with the man in the produce section. I told him I wanted to be wild and passionate. He suggested I purchase some passion fruit.* [Show it to the kids and then take a bite. Then transform from quiet monotone voice to energetic and excited, full of passion, and exclaim with a loud voice: *"AWESOME!!!!"*] [Give some to the senior pastor and say, *"Maybe we should give these out to everyone before the worship service! That would change things around here – man, we'd rock this place!!!"* You know, I did some research on Internet [hold up the paper], *because everyone knows that the Internet doesn't lie!* [This elicited some laughs from the adults.] *I read from the article: "Passion fruit got its name from Spanish missionaries who thought that the flower of the passion fruit reminded them of Jesus' crucifixion – it looked like a hammer, nails, and a crown of thorns." Hmmn . . . that's interesting. What on earth does a hammer, nails, and a crown of thorns/crucifixion have to do with "passion"?* [Ask them.] *Everything! If someone was so crazy about you that they'd die for you – now that's passion! Was Jesus passionate? Did He have passion? Oh yes – He had so much passion that He suffered and died for us. Now THAT'S passion! Let's pray.*

Prayer

Lord, thank You so much for Your passion for us. May we understand and receive Your passion, so that we'd have passion for one another. Amen.

Pass the Ball

Scripture

Matthew 16:25
"For whoever desires to save his life will lose it, but whoever loses his life for My sake will find it."

Luke 12:32-34
"Do not fear, little flock, for it is your Father's good pleasure to give you the kingdom. Sell what you have and give alms; provide yourselves money bags which do not grow old, a treasure in the heavens that does not fail, where no thief approaches nor moth destroys. For where your treasure is, there your heart will be also."

1 Timothy 6:17-19
"Command those who are rich in this present age not to be haughty, nor to trust in uncertain riches but in the living God, who gives us richly all things to enjoy. Let them do good, that they may be rich in good works, ready to give, willing to share, storing up for themselves a good foundation for the time to come, that they may lay hold on eternal life."

Big Idea

Hell is where you hold onto and hoard what you have in fear; heaven is where you can freely give away what you have in joy, trusting in the Father's goodness.

Materials

Large ball.

Overview

The first day I started at Lookout Mountain Community Church back in 1994, Peter (the Senior Pastor) took me out to lunch. In the course of our conversation, he said something I've never forgotten: *"People in our church community (including myself) are rich – they are wealthy. They've got a lot. Thus one of their greatest needs is to give themselves away. I believe that one of my primary jobs here is to help them give themselves away."* This has stayed with me and has informed my thinking in a profound way. We are most miserable when we are hanging on, hoarding. But to empty ourselves and lose ourselves for Jesus – this is where we find *life*, and where we find *joy*.

I've heard it said that all sin has its roots in the suspicion that God is not good. In the parable of the talents, the steward who was chastised was the one who found his master "to be a hard man" and buried his talent in the ground in fear (Matt. 25:24-25). Every good and perfect gift comes from above, from the Father of lights (James 1:17). To have a "heavenly posture" is to have a posture of the soul which is "upward and outward," looking up to God with arms open wide, ready to receive and to give freely to others. In contrast, to have a "hellish posture" is to have a posture of the soul that is "downward and inward," looking only into the self and consumed with self, where trust and joy in the "Father of lights" has been extinguished. In Scripture, a frequent metaphor for sin and idolatry is to be "bent over," no longer looking upward, and becoming like an animal (cf. Jeremiah 2:27 "For they have turned their back to Me, and not their face;" Romans 1:22-23 "Professing to be wise they became fools, and changed the glory of the incorruptible God into an image made like corruptible man – and birds and four-footed animals and creeping things.")

Sermon

I need four or five volunteers. Let's go up on the stage and sit in a circle, and let's have some fun and play a game of "catch." [Begin passing the ball to each other, exhorting them to pass it faster and faster. Whistle the tune "Sweet Georgia Brown" to make it fun.] *Woo hoo! Isn't this fun!* [After doing this for about 30 seconds or so, stop the "fun" by holding onto the ball, and turning your back to the kids while holding on tightly to the ball. At this, the kids will begin to become sad or complain.] *What's the matter? Aren't you having fun? Why aren't you having fun?* [The children will yell out, "Because you're holding onto the ball!"] *But the ball is MINE . . . it's MY OWN! My PRECIOUS (I played a little humor here off the character Gollum in* Lord of the Rings.) [At this point one little girl, being bored, got up and walked off the stage, not wanting to "play the game" anymore. The congregation laughed, and it played right into my message.]*Oh no . . . it looks like she's not having any fun . . . it's not fun anymore when you hold onto the ball, huh. That kind of reminds me of the difference between heaven and hell. I think hell is where everyone is holding onto the ball, afraid that they might lose it and never get it again. But heaven is where everyone passes the ball when they get it, bringing joy to everyone. Now let me ask you one more question: If Jesus was here, sitting in our circle, and I held onto the ball, how do you think He would feel? What do you think He would say? Do you think He would yell and scream at me and kick me out of the circle?* [One child said, "No – He would just say to pass the ball." Another child said, "He would be sad."] *Yes – I think Jesus would be sad, because I was in so much fear and I was robbing everyone of joy. And do you know what He would do? I think He'd do everything He could to take away my fear, and help me to trust Him so I could share the ball. Maybe He'd even die for me. That's what Jesus is like, isn't it? He's pretty cool!*

Prayer

Lord, help us to trust in Your goodness; for when we hang on and try to save our lives we lose it, but when we lose our lives for You we'll find it. Help us, Jesus. Amen.

Pentecost

Scripture

Ezekiel 36:26-27
"I will give you a new heart and put a new spirit within you; I will take the heart of stone out of your flesh and give you a heart of flesh. I will put My Spirit within you and cause you to walk in My statutes, and you will keep My judgments and do them." – cf. Jeremiah 31:31-33

Acts 2:1-4
"When the Day of Pentecost had fully come, they were with one accord in one place. And suddenly there came a sound from heaven, as of a rushing mighty wind, and it filled the whole house where they were sitting. Then there appeared to them divided tongues, as of fire, and one sat upon each of them. And they were all filled with the Holy Spirit and began to speak with other tongues, as the Spirit gave them utterance."

Materials

Two "stone" tablets with the 10 Commandments written on them. (You can use foam or wood and spray paint the tablets, and then use a marker to write out some Hebrew word – or you can carve them if you want to be creative.)

Big Idea

The Good News of the New Covenant is that God has come inside of us and has written His very law into our hearts, so that what is *most true* about us is that we *love* to do His will.

Overview

The Jewish celebration of Pentecost was like a big wedding celebration. {Pente" means "50" – and Pentecost occurs 50 days after Passover. It was also known as the "Feast of Weeks" (7 days x 7 weeks = 49 days – and the feast was celebrated the day after these 49 days of waiting.) See Leviticus 23:15 ff. This is pretty cool, in that Jesus told the disciples to "wait" in Jerusalem for the coming of the Holy Spirit.

Pentecost also consisted of the "Feast of the First-fruits" – where pilgrims came to Jerusalem to bring the first-fruits of their early spring harvest. So in Jerusalem at this time, there were thousands of pilgrims from all nations and nationalities – again, it was a big celebration with lots of guests coming in from out of town. But the basic idea of "Pentecost" was that it was a celebration of the giving of the law to Moses on Mt. Sinai. The Jews saw that event as a kind of wedding, where God gave the law to His bride (Israel) as a gift – not to "restrict" them, but to protect and provide for them. The "law" was, in essence, His wedding contract. When Moses was up on Sinai, there was fire and smoke on top of the mountain – which was kind of like a canopy. I believe this is where the concept of a canopy at Jewish weddings originated. The Israelites were instructed by Moses to wait for him to come down. But they refused to wait, and fashioned the golden calf. When Moses returned, he shattered the two tablets of the law. This is the meaning of why at Jewish weddings to this day, the wedding celebration begins by breaking a glass – to remind them that the bride didn't wait for the coming of her groom back then.

But here's the point: Back when God gave the law to Israel, there was fire and thunder on the mountain. God asked the people to wait, and then God wrote the law with His very finger on the tablets of stone. But in the New Testament, at Pentecost (which was a celebration of remembrance of this very event), God once again asked the disciples to wait – and this time, He came with a loud rushing sound and "tongues of fire." But instead of writing on tablets of stone, with the very same finger He wrote His law in their hearts! (cf. Ezekiel 36:25-27) . . . which He continues to do to this day.

Sermon

Hold up the stone tablet and ask, *"Does anyone know what this is? Remember when God gave Moses the Law – and the 10 Commandments? How did He do it?"* [Moses went up on Mt. Sinai, there was fire and thunder, and then God wrote the Law in tablets of stone – like this – with His very finger!]

"Does anyone know what holiday it is this weekend? It's called 'Pentecost.' Does anyone know what Pentecost is?" [Explain to them the concept of Pentecost – i.e. that it occurs 50 days after Passover, and it commemorates when God gave the Law to His people – His Bride – on Mt. Sinai – where there was a canopy of smoke, and God asked the people to wait, and then God came with fire and wrote the Law on tablets of stone – that probably looked something like this.] *"Let me ask you: Did the Israelites wait? NO, they made the golden calf, and then do you remember what Moses did? He threw down the tablets of stone and they shattered."*

[Then, over 1,300 years later, there was a very important Pentecost: 50 days after Jesus was sacrificed as THE Passover lamb, the disciples were all waiting in Jerusalem – in the "Upper Room" – kind of reminds you of how Moses was "up" on the mountain, and God once again came to His people with fire and the loud sound of a mighty wind – and with His very same finger He once again gives us the law . . . but this time, instead of writing it in stone, He wrote it on their hearts! And that's what He does with us.] *"When we believe in Jesus, the Holy Spirit comes inside of us and writes the Law in our hearts! That means that we really WANT to obey and follow God – and that's what will bring us the most joy in life. And when we disobey God, we're going to be miserable, because we're not doing what our true heart deep down really wants to do!"*

Prayer

Let's pray and listen to what the prophet Ezekiel said: "I will give you a new heart and put a new spirit within you, I will take the heart of stone out of your flesh and give you a heart of flesh. I will put My Spirit within you, and cause you to walk in My ways." Thank You, Jesus, that You have given us a new heart and that You live inside us. Thank You for making us entirely new! Amen.

People and Purpose

Scripture

James 2:15-16

"If a brother or sister is naked and destitute of daily food, and one of you says to them, 'Depart in peace, be warmed and be filled,' but you do not give them the things which are needed for the body, what does it profit?

John 5:39-42

"You search the Scriptures, for in them you think you have eternal life; and these are they which testify of Me. But you are not willing to come to Me that you may have life. I do not receive honor from men. But I know you, that you do not have the love of God in you."

Big Idea

Jesus never asks us to commit to a purpose at the expense of a person.

Materials

Find a document or a declaration against hunger (I found one easily on the Internet – it was an "American Declaration against Hunger") You will also need a power-bar or some kind of nutritious piece of food. You will also need to arrange to have another adult be a part of the children's sermon.

Overview

So often in ministry it's easy to become so consumed with a "cause" or a "purpose" that we forget the very people we're ministering alongside in the cause – and risk "using" them or forgetting them. With Jesus it was never "either/or." Jesus definitely had a purpose – to die for the sins of the world and to bring the kingdom of God to mankind – but He never did it at the expense of people; on the contrary, He sacrificed Himself for the very people His "cause" was about.

152

Sermon

[For this I arranged for Mike, one of our other pastors, to interrupt me continually as I read from the "Declaration against Hunger." He was to play the part of a hungry person desperately in need of food.] *Good Morning! Did you all have breakfast this morning? Are you feeling pretty full? That's good. But do you know that there are millions of children all over the world who are starving and dying because of a lack of food or proper nourishment? I was thinking about this and I figured I better do something about it. So I got on the Internet and I did a lot of research on hunger, and I discovered that there's not only hunger in the world's developing countries like you'd expect, but there's also a lot of children who are hungry right here in this country! Do you believe that? Let me read to you from this "Declaration against Hunger."* [Project it up on the visual screen if you have one; or just hold it up and read from it.] As I began reading, Mike interrupted me every 5 or 10 seconds, saying something like *"Hey Aram, I see that you're talking about hunger this morning . . . hey, I didn't have any breakfast this morning, and I'm really hungry."*

"Mike, Mike," I replied. *"Can't you see that I'm busy? I have a very important cause I'm working on right now, to stamp out world hunger. I can't help you right now – could you please be seated?"* I returned to reading from the document; then Mike interrupted me again – *"Hey Aram, I really mean it – I REALLY AM hungry. I haven't eaten in days, and I'm starving . . . can you help me?"* To which I respond, *"Mike, I already told you once – this is NOT the time . . . I'm busy with this very important work in my life, addressing the needs of the hungry – right here in our very own country! So could you please stop interrupting me?"* I then resumed reading from the document and once again was interrupted. *"Aram, I REALLY, REALLY, REALLY AM hungry! Can't you see I haven't eaten in days? I really could use some food right now. Please help me!"* To which I responded, *"Good night! I can't get two words in without you interrupting me! And now I'm just about out of time with my children's sermon, and I haven't even been able to read this important document on hunger to the kids. Thanks a lot!"*

OK, kids, I guess we'll need to close in prayer. [At this point I looked at them and it was obvious they were upset and perplexed.].*What? Why are you looking at me like that? What's the matter?* [At this the children responded, "You were talking about hunger and Mike was hungry and you didn't help him!] *Oh . . . you mean I was so caught up in my "cause" that I couldn't see the hungry person right in front of my eyes? Oh . . . that IS a problem, isn't it? Maybe I should help Mike, huh?* [At this point I tossed Mike a power bar.] *Here you go, Mike. I think sometimes that's what we do: We become so concerned about a problem that we get really busy and we miss the opportunities right before our very eyes that God sends our way to help. That's a problem, isn't it? We better pray.*

Prayer

Lord, help us not to get so busy and wrapped up in a cause that we miss the very people You bring into our lives that need our love and care. Help us to see where You are calling us to help and love others who are in need. Amen.

Pickled

Scripture

2 Corinthians 5:17
"Therefore, if anyone is in Christ, he is a new creation; old things have passed away; behold, all things have become new."

Galatians 2:20
"I have been crucified with Christ; it is no longer I who live, but Christ lives in me."

Colossians 3:9-10
"Do not lie to one another, since you have put off the old man with his deeds, and have put on the new man who is renewed in knowledge according to the image of Him who created him."

Big Idea

The Spirit makes us a new person – we are no longer who we were (though we bear the same resemblance on the outside).

Materials

Small cucumber, glass jar, vinegar, jar of seasoned pickles (e.g. Vlasic or something familiar).

Overview

Herein lies the essence of the New Covenant. Because of the indwelling of the Spirit of God through faith in Christ, I am a "new person," I am no longer the person I once was. Though I may look like the "old person," and even act and live like him (when I forget God and live out of my flesh – my "old self"); fundamentally, at the core, I am a new person. What is *most* true about me is that I long to worship and honor God and love Him and love others. Because of "Christ in me," this is what is *most* true about me. That is a staggering thought.

Sermon

[Hold up a small cucumber.] *What's this? Yes, it's a cucumber. Ever eat a cucumber?* [Take a bite of the cucumber; or perhaps offer one of the kids a bite.] *Tastes pretty good, doesn't it? Cucumbers are good to put in your salad, or to eat in a sandwich. Now, let me ask you this...* [take out empty jar and a bottle of vinegar; begin pouring the vinegar into the empty jar; place the cucumber into the jar and close the lid.] *What if I were to take this cucumber, and dip it into this jar of vinegar, and leave it in there, say, for a few months. What would happen? What would become of the cucumber?* [All the kids yelled out, "It would become a pickle!"] *At this moment, pull out a brand-name jar of pickles and open it.] Yes! It would become a pickle!!! It still looks like a cucumber, but it's a lot different, isn't it? It has a whole new flavor! So even though it may look like a cucumber on the outside, it's no longer a cucumber. It's been transformed into a pickle!* [Eat one of the pickles.] *Wow – it's a whole new thing! It's no longer what it was – even though it still looks like a cucumber. That reminds me of us – when we believe in Jesus. Even though we might still look the same, the Holy Spirit comes into us and He permeates us – and gives us a whole new flavor. And other people will begin to notice – that even though we may look the same on the outside, they'll be able to see that we're a much different person on the inside. Because Jesus is inside of us and He's filling us with His Spirit – so we're no longer who we were. Isn't that cool?*

Prayer

Lord, thank You for changing us from the inside out. Thank You for filling us with Your Spirit so that we're a new person! Help us to believe that, so that we might live like who You are making us to be. Amen.

Red Rover

Scripture

Psalm 147:2-5
"The Lord builds Jerusalem; He gathers together the outcasts of Israel. He heals the brokenhearted and He binds up their wounds. He counts the number of the stars; He calls them all by name. Great is our Lord, and mighty in power; His understanding is infinite."

Isaiah 40:26
"Lift up your eyes on high, and see who has created these things, who brings out their host by number; He calls them all by name, by the greatness of His might and the strength of His power; not one is missing."

John 10:3-4
"To Him the doorkeeper opens, and the sheep hear His voice; and He calls His own sheep by name and leads them out. And when He brings out His own sheep, He goes before them; and the sheep follow Him, for they know His voice."

3 John 14
"But I hope to see you shortly, and we shall speak face to face. Peace to you. Our friends greet you. Greet the friends by name."

Big Idea

We all long to be known by our names. God knows us intimately, and calls us by our name.

Materials

No materials needed, but you will need to recruit about seven of the children to help you do this.

Overview

My friend and colleague Mike preached a sermon on our longing to be called and known by our names. He used the text from John 10:3-4. He began the sermon by describing a familiar – and oftentimes painful – memory from childhood, usually in gym class or on the playground, when two kids would choose their teams. Usually the "popular" and athletic kids would get chosen first; and those chosen last would be branded as "losers." He contrasted this with a more positive memory, that being when they played the game of "Red Rover." In Red Rover you also longed to be called by name. But unlike other games, in Red Rover there were never any individual "losers" – for if you broke through the line, you could take another kid and go back, to the cheers of your original team. But if you were "caught" by the other side, unable to break through, you were welcomed into their fold and now a part of their team. And eventually, everyone was called by name. And everybody would win. God calls each of us by name. We are not small and insignificant to Him. He knew us and chose us from "before the foundation of the earth" (Ephesians 1:4). He calls each one of us by name. We are not objects to Him, and He is not some kind of impersonal power or "force." God intimately knows us; and we long to be known – by Him, and by others.

Sermon

How many of you like the game, "Red Rover?" [Many raised their hands.] *I love Red Rover – in fact, I'd like to play a game right now. I need some volunteers – who would like to play with me?* [Many again raised their hands; I chose seven children and invited them up on the stage with me, where I formed two lines (i.e. "sides") with me being on one of the sides with three of the children.] *Okay – I'll start: Red Rover, Red Rover, send human entity number three right over!* [The children looked dumbfounded.] *I thought you guys knew how to play this game! Let me try again: Red Rover, Red Rover, send human entity number three right over!* [They still had a look of confusion on their faces. At this point I explained and showed the opposing team that the third person from the end was "human entity number three."] I then pointed at this little girl and said, *"You're human entity number three! Come on over!"* She still had a befuddled look on her face. Just as I was going to choose one of the other children, she bolted from her line and ran to ours, and she was so small that she went right underneath everyone's arms. At this point (this actually happened) she looked out into the congregation where her mother was sitting and yelled out, "Look mom – I did it!" The congregation burst out in laughter and applause. *Yes, you did it! Okay, now that you've got the hang of it, let's try it again: Red Rover Red Rover, send human entity number one right over!* [They caught on this time, and the first child in the line came bolting over to our side.] *Now let me ask you: How did it feel being called a "human entity?"* [The kids responded, "Weird," and some said, "Not good."] *You don't like being called a "human entity, do you?"* [No!] *You don't like being called a number, do you?* [No!] *You're not some kind of thing or object, right? You're a person, with a name, right? Don't you love being called by your name? I think that's the best part of playing Red Rover – to hear your name called. You know the Bible says that God calls each of us by our name. Isn't that cool? That's because we're not things or objects, and God is not some kind of "power" or "force." God is a person – and His name is?* [At this they yelled out, JESUS!] *Let's pray!*

Prayer

Lord, thank You that You are not some kind of impersonal force or power, but You are a person, and You call each one of us by name. Thank You for loving us like that. And we pray this in YOUR name, Jesus, Amen.

Ruler Reality

Scripture

Romans 1:25
". . . who exchanged the truth of God for the lie. . . ."

Isaiah 44:20
"A deceived heart has turned him aside; and he cannot deliver his soul, nor say, 'Is there not a lie in my right hand?'"

Big Idea

Heaven is where we say, "Thy will be done." Hell is where God says, "Thy will be done" (i.e. we exchange His reality for our own reality).

Materials

Two wooden rulers. Make sure they are all wood, and do not have metal edges (you will need to break one of them in half).

Overview

Idolatry is the essence of our rebellion against God. It is where we exchange (what I call) "capital R" Reality for our own, smaller realities ("small r" reality). We rewrite truth to make our lives work – in essence, becoming our own God. This is why God says in Romans 1:23 that we ". . . changed the *glory* of the incorruptible God into an image make like corruptible man. . . ." The word "glory" in Hebrew conjures up the idea of scales – i.e. to "glorify God" means to "give weight" to God. It's what gives our lives *substance*. When we exchange this glory for our own, we (like C.S. Lewis would say) become "shadows" – we become "less" – and lose our substance.

Sermon

I need two volunteers!" [Pick one adult – preferably someone tall and well known; and then pick one small child.] *Now, I have a question for you: Who do you think is taller? Well, let's measure him* (use one of the 12-inch wooden rulers and measure the adult.) *Now, let's measure _____* (the child). [Take the ruler and break it in half, and then measure the child, pretending that the small ruler is now measuring in feet. Count the "feet" out loud. The child should register slightly taller than the adult. At this point, the congregation broke out in laughter, especially as the child registered a look of pride on his face!] *Well, what do you think? Is (the child) really taller than (the adult)? What's the problem?* ("You broke the ruler!") *I made my own ruler, didn't I? And that's not a true ruler, is it?*

Now, let me ask you this: Who is the ruler of our lives? Of the world? (God!) *He is THE ruler, isn't He? Now, what do you think would happen if we don't like His rules – like "Don't steal" or "Don't murder" or "Don't lie." What do you think would happen to the world? There would be lots of trouble, wouldn't there? Everyone would be making up their own rules. Everyone would do whatever they wanted, and there would be total chaos!*

Do you know that God is our ruler – and He is a good ruler – the best ruler! And if we don't like His rules, and we do our own thing, we're going to get ourselves into a lot of trouble!

Prayer

Lord, help us and stop us when we go off and create our own "rulers" – our own reality. Help us to live according to Your truth – even when we might not like it; because You love us and know what's best for us. Amen.

St. Patrick's Day Prayer

Scripture

Hebrews 13:5-6

"He Himself has said, 'I will never leave you, nor forsake you,' so that we may confidently say, 'The Lord is my helper, I will not be afraid. What shall man do to me?'"

Ephesians 3: 16-19

". . . that He would grant you, according to the riches of His glory, to be strengthened with might through His Spirit in the inner man, that Christ may dwell in your hearts through faith; that you, being rooted and grounded in love, may be able to comprehend with all the saints what is the width and length and depth and height – to know the love of Christ. . . ."

Psalm 139:7

"Where can I go from Your Spirit? Or where can I flee from Your presence?"

Big Idea

The "Shield of St. Patrick" comforts us when feeling worried or anxious by reminding us that Jesus is everywhere – and in every circumstance.

Materials

If you have a projection screen, have a slide with the Shield of St. Patrick on it (at left) – with a green colored background. Also, make copies of the prayer to hand out to each child. Have the prayer inside a "shield" – on green paper. And it would also be good to be wearing some green articles of clothing!

The Shield of St. Patrick

Christ be with me, Christ within me,
Christ behind me, Christ before me,
Christ beside me, Christ to win me;
Christ to comfort and restore me.

Christ beneath me, Christ above me,
Christ in quiet, Christ in danger,
Christ in hearts of all that love me,
Christ in mouth of friend and stranger.

Overview

Most of us view St. Patrick's Day as a day to wear green and recognize and celebrate the Irish. However, the story of St. Patrick is one worth looking at more closely. Patrick was originally from Great Britain, possibly Wales (he was the son of a priest, Calpornius, a name which some speculate was Italian – possibly making him half Italian!) By the age of 16 he was taken into captivity into Ireland, and was enslaved there. It was during this time that he found Jesus. He later went back to Ireland to serve as a missionary. The "Shield" or "Breastplate" of St. Patrick is a beautiful prayer that has been attributed to him – though the certainty of his authorship is the subject of some debate. The "shield" printed above is but an excerpt from this incredibly beautiful prayer or hymn. It speaks of the all-encompassing presence and love of Christ.

Sermon

We're continuing in the season of Lent, which, as we said before, is the time of preparation leading us to Easter. And this week we have a special holiday coming up . . . does anyone know what that special day is? (Point to green parts of your clothing as you're saying this!) Some of the kids will likely shout out the proper answer. *That's right – St. Patrick's Day! But who was St. Patrick? What's he famous for? Was he famous for discovering Lucky Charms cereal?* (No!) *Was he famous for discovering four-leaf clovers?* (No!) *Was he famous for putting green dye in assorted beverages?* (No!) *Was he famous for the Blarney Stone?* (No!) *Actually, one of the things I think St. Patrick was most famous for was a beautiful prayer he wrote. It's called the "Shield of St. Patrick." Now, let me ask: What does a shield do?* (It protects you from harm.) *When you're in battle, you really need a shield to protect you, don't you? And it gives you courage and comfort when you're feeling scared. Let's look at this prayer which became known as the shield of St. Patrick.* (If you have a projection screen, project this at this point.) *Let's read it together.* (Have the children and adults read it together in unison.) *Isn't that beautiful? Doesn't that give you courage – knowing that Jesus is everywhere around you when you feel afraid? I'm going to give you each a "shield" of St. Patrick. Maybe you can put it up in your room – so you can pray it when you feel afraid.* (Hand them out after prayer.) *Let's pray.*

Prayer

Lord, thank You for your presence in our world, and in our lives. Thank You that You are always with us, and will never leave us or abandon us. Please give us faith to believe in Your goodness and presence in times of trouble, that we may be encouraged. Amen.

Shout!

Scripture

Ephesians 1:4-6
"Just as He chose us in Him before the foundation of the world, that we should be holy and without blame before Him in love, having predestined us to adoption as sons by Jesus Christ to Himself, according to the good pleasure of His will, to the praise of the glory of His grace. . . ."

Ephesians 2:7
"So that in the ages to come He might show the exceeding riches of His grace in His kindness toward us in Christ Jesus."

Romans 5:20-21;6:1-2
"Moreover the law entered that the offense might abound. But where sin abounded, grace abounded all the more, so that as sin reigned in death, even so grace might reign through righteousness to eternal life through Jesus Christ our Lord. What shall we say then? Shall we continue in sin that grace may abound? Certainly not! How shall we who died to sin live any longer in it?"

Big Idea

Without sin and "The Fall," there would have been aspects of God's character and nature, namely His grace, mercy, and compassion, that we would have never known.

Materials

Spray bottle of "Shout" stain remover; white shirt, catsup.

Overview

This children's sermon is perhaps one of the most deeply theological I ever attempted. It is an amazing thing to think about: that without the presence and knowledge of sin, there would have never been an opportunity to know and experience the grace and mercy of God. Yet that is precisely what these verses from Ephesians and Romans imply. And just as Paul anticipated the logical next question in Romans 6:1, when we come to grasp the overarching purposes of God – i.e. "to show us the exceeding riches of His grace in kindness toward us in Christ," we are left to wonder similarly: "Well, should we then go ahead and sin so that God can reveal more of His grace?" The mystery is indeed sobering and profound: that while it is indeed God's intention to reveal the riches of His grace toward us in Christ, it comes at the ultimate cost – the cost of Him bearing the entirety of our sin upon Himself. To continue in sin is to continue to pound more and more nails into the Son of God. As "deep" as these thoughts appear, what was incredible to me (judging by the kids' response to my questions) was that *they got it.*

Sermon

[Hold up bottle of Shout stain remover.] *Does anyone know what this is?* [A few yelled out, "It's Shout!"] *Yes – it's Shout! What does it do?* [Many yelled out that it was some kind of cleaner; one or two said that it removed stains.] *Do you think it's good? Do you think it's powerful?* [The kids shouted out, "Yes!"] *Well, how do you know? How do you know that it's good and powerful and can really get out stains?* [The kids thought for a few moments.] *You would need a stain to reveal whether it was a good and powerful stain remover, right? Because without a stain, you would never know how good and powerful this Shout really is, right? Well, it just so happens that I'm wearing this nice white shirt today; maybe we can stain this nice white shirt and see whether this Shout really is good and powerful.* [At this point I took out a large bottle of catsup. I then squirted a little on my white shirt, and then rubbed it into the shirt with my finger.] *Let's see if this stuff really is good!* [I then sprayed the Shout onto the stain and began rubbing it into the stain; and all the stain came out.] *Wow! Check this out! The Shout really is good and powerful!*

Now let me ask you another question. Is God forgiving? ["Yes!" they all shouted.] *Is He merciful?* ["Yes!" they all shouted.] *Is He full of grace toward us?* ["Yes!" they all shouted again.] *Well, how do you know? How do you know that God is forgiving? That He is merciful?* [There was pretty much silence at this point.] *The only way you can know if God is forgiving is if He forgives you, right? And the only way He can forgive you is if there's something to forgive – a sin to forgive, right?* [They all said, "Yes."] *Well then, it seems to me that the only way we'd know if God is forgiving and gracious and merciful is if we sin, right?* [At this point there was a look of befuddlement on the children's faces – as there should have been. Their befuddlement indicated that they were indeed getting my point.] *So – if the only way we could know that the forgiveness and mercy and grace of God is if we sin, should we go on sinning, so God can show us more grace?* [At this point, many of the kids shouted out, "NO!"] *No! Because the incredible and wonderful and amazing thing is that Jesus had to die for all of our sin; and what's really amazing is that He took all our punishment on Himself . . . and He did all of this in order to reveal His grace and kindness and mercy to us! Isn't that amazing? Doesn't that make you want to worship Him? Let's pray . . .*

Prayer

Lord, thank You that, indeed, where sin abounded, grace abounded all the more. Thank You for Your grace and mercy toward us. You took all our sins and put them on Yourself – in order that You might reveal Your incredible grace toward us. You are amazing. Amen.

Signs

Scripture

Matthew 12:38-39
"Then some of the scribes and Pharisees answered, saying, 'Teacher, we want to see a sign from You.' But He answered and said to them, 'An evil and adulterous generation seeks after a sign, and no sign will be given to it except the sign of the prophet Jonah.'"

1 Corinthians 1: 22-23
"For Jews request a sign, and Greeks seek after wisdom; but we preach Christ crucified, to the Jews a stumbling block and to the Greeks foolishness. . . ."

Big Idea

We seek signs from God to help us and reassure us; but Jesus calls us to be a sign, sacrificing ourselves for the sake of others.

Materials

A large traffic sign (e.g. a yellow sign with an arrow works great for this). If you can't find one, you can make one using poster board.

Overview

The line is fine between genuinely longing for God's leading, and faithlessly demanding a sign. We all seek clarity in our decisionmaking, and guidance and confirmation of our choices. Yet this sometimes masks a subtle – yet very real – desire to walk by sight . . . and not by faith. Trust, despite the absence of signs, is a great gift we can offer to Jesus. And an even greater gift we can offer Him is to choose to be a sign instead of seeking one. There is no greater sign than the cross. The sign of Jonah was a type of this kind of sign – one man offering His life so that others might live.* We are called to carry our own crosses – as signs of His love in the world.

Sermon

[Hold up sign.] *I brought something with me this morning . . . do you know what this is?* [One child yelled out, "A stolen traffic sign!"] *It's a sign! See the arrow? It tells you where to go. Wouldn't it be great if God would give us signs like this? You know – signs where He'd tell us what to do, or where to go, or to answer all our questions and prayers? A lot of us would really like signs from God. But do you know what really makes Jesus happy? Not looking for signs, but that we would* **be** *a sign!*

A lot of people in Jesus' day wanted signs – but Jesus said that no sign would be given to them except the sign of Jonah. Do you remember what happened to Jonah, when he was on the boat and the storm came? [Most kids know the story of Jonah, and will shout out answers here.] *A huge storm came upon the boat, and Jonah offered to be thrown off the boat to save the ship and the rest of the people on the boat. And when the storm continued to rage, do you remember what happened? They threw him off the boat! And what happened next? The storm stopped, and the rest of the crew was saved! So, one man offered to be thrown into the storm and die, so that everyone on the boat could live! Hmmm . . . that kind of sounds familiar, doesn't it? Jesus said that was the sign of Jonah. No wonder nobody wants to be a sign! That would require sacrificing your life – so that others could live. That's the sign of Jesus. And He is thrilled when His children are willing to be signs like that. Let's pray.*

*I'm aware that some see the "sign of Jonah" as referring primarily to the time he spent in the belly of the whale before coming back to "life" again. But as far as the children are concerned, this perspective on the "sign of Jonah" – i.e. that one man would lay down his life for others – is just as significant.

Prayer

Lord, forgive us for always demanding signs from You. Please help us to be a sign of Your love in the world, sacrificing ourselves so that others might live. Amen.

Tabasco I: Fire & Thirst

Scripture

Psalm 107:5-6
"Hungry and thirsty, their soul fainted in them. Then they cried out to the Lord in their trouble . . ."

Isaiah 55:1
"Ho! Everyone who thirsts, come to the waters . . ."

John 7:37
"On the last day, that great day of the feast, Jesus stood and cried out, saying, 'If anyone thirsts, let him come to Me and drink. He who believes in Me, as the Scripture has said, out of his hear will flow rivers of living water.'"

Big Idea

Trials create thirst for God.

Materials

Pitcher of water, drinking glass, bottle of Tabasco sauce, bowl of sugar, spoon.

Overview

In all my years of doing children's sermons, this one came to be most renowned. For years after this sermon, people talked about it, razzed me about it, and even gave me gifts because of it (Tabasco T-shirts, Tabasco candies, Tabasco magnets, Tabasco ties, etc.). To do this right, you will need to be courageous and drink a lot of Tabasco! I recommend bringing some pain reliever with you (that afternoon I had a killer headache from drinking the stuff). An added benefit to this sermon is that it gave rise to a second "Tabasco" sermon, because of what happened later (see Tabasco II). The sermon conveys a truth that is simple, yet profoundly difficult to embrace: that the fiery ordeals that come upon us can give us a thirst for God that usually is not there when things are smooth and sweet. In this sense, we can give thanks for times of desert and fiery ordeals in our lives – for they increase our yearning for living water.

Sermon

Begin by eating some sugar from a spoon. Talk about how sometimes life is sweet, where everything is going pretty well – e.g., you're getting along with your friends, you're healthy, and life is good. At this point, pour some water in the glass and drink a *small* sip of water.

"*But sometimes life is not so sweet – sometimes life is more like this.*" (Hold up large bottle of Tabasco sauce) *Life is like FIRE! With trials and problems and suffering!* (Then hold your head back, lift up the bottle, and pour copious amounts of the sauce in your mouth. The more you pour, the better the effect; and the greater the headache later – but that's the price you need to pay!)

After I finished drinking the sauce, I stopped for a moment and just looked at the kids. Then, very abruptly, I let out a loud shriek and ran for the water pitcher. I desperately poured one glass, and downed it. Then I poured another glass, and downed it. Then I tossed the glass aside and I lifted the pitcher and began downing the water right from the pitcher (you will have no trouble doing this, as you will need every ounce of that water to put out the fire in your mouth!)

After settling things down a bit, I then asked this question: "*When was I more thirsty – when everything was sweet, or when I had the hot stuff? Jesus once said that He was like "living water." I think Jesus is a lot like this water: when life is sweet and everything is going well, usually we're not all that thirsty. But when the trials and fires come, we get really thirsty and we need Him and we drink the most. So God sometimes brings trials into our lives to make us thirst for Him!*"

Prayer

Lord, sometimes it's hard when You allow trials and suffering in our lives. Yet we also know, Lord, that when everything is going great, we are often quick to forget You. So thank You for the trials as well as the good times, Lord, and for bringing things into our lives that deepen our thirst for You. Amen.

Tabasco II: Faith that Works

Scripture

James 2:14, 17-18

"What does it profit, my brethren, if someone says he has faith but does not have works? Can faith save him . . . Thus also faith by itself, if it does not have works, is dead. But someone will say, 'You have faith, and I have works.' Show me your faith without your works, and I will show you my faith by my works."

Big Idea

Faith without works is dead.

Materials

Large bottle of Tabasco sauce, pitcher of water, cups.

Overview

This sermon arose inadvertently from the previous Tabasco sermon, and provided a great opportunity to teach on the nature of faith. After my Tabasco fiasco, word got back to me that many (I was surprised how many) had doubts that I really drank Tabasco sauce; many accused me of using water with food coloring (the blasphemers!). So I decided that the next weekend I would go after those of our congregation who were "of such little faith!"

Sermon

I have some unfinished business from last week that I need to conduct this morning! For it has come to my attention that some of you – mostly you adults – had serious "doubts" about my children's sermon last weekend. It seems that many of you did not believe that I actually drank real Tabasco sauce – and murmurs have reached my ears that I instead drank water with food coloring! Is this true? O ye of little faith? Well, let me now ask you adults: How many of you doubted my act of supreme sacrifice and courage last weekend, and believe that what I really drank was something far more tame – something like water with food coloring?

When someone raised his hand, I then "called him out:" "So, Leo, *you say you believe that what I really drank last weekend, from this very bottle, was not Tabasco sauce, but water with food coloring? Is that what you believe? Well then, if you really believe this, prove it to me and show me by your actions what you believe in your heart: I want you to come on up here and take a nice, big, swig of this "colored water"! Come on – you should have nothing to fear!* [At our church we had two identical morning worship services at the time. As I recall, at one service, several raised their hands, but no one had the guts to come up. This worked out great: I pointed out that several "said" they believed it was food coloring, but their actions did not back it up – therefore their faith was dead. However, at the other service, "Leo" took up my challenge and came up – and he guzzled down huge quantities of the Tabasco! It was hysterical. And I commended him for his faith to back up what he believed to be true, while still chastising him for his lack of faith in me the previous week.]

Prayer

Lord, help us to live out what we believe in our hearts. Make us into people who demonstrate our faith by our actions – people of integrity. In Your name, Amen.

Tape Measure Job

Scripture

1 Samuel 16:7
"But the Lord said to Samuel, 'Do not look at his appearance or at the height of his stature, because I have rejected him; for God sees not as man sees, for man looks at the outward appearance, but the Lord looks at the heart.'"

John 7:24
"Do not judge according to appearance, but judge with righteous judgment."

Romans 8:1
"There is therefore now no condemnation to those who are in Christ Jesus, who do not walk according to the flesh, but according to the Spirit."

2 Corinthians 5:16-17
"Therefore, from now on, we regard no one according to the flesh. Even though we have known Christ according to the flesh, yet we now know Him thus no longer. Therefore, if anyone is in Christ, he is a new creation; old things have passed away; behold, all things have become new."

Materials

Tape measure, legal pad of paper, pen.

Big Idea

God measures us according to Jesus, not according to how we look, or how we act, or how much we know.

Overview

Having "eyes that see" is a big theme in the Bible. And it lies at the heart of the New Covenant. If the New Covenant is true, then we are not to define others according to their gifts, strengths, and abilities; nor their weaknesses, wounded-ness, or struggles. Yet, if we're honest, we do this all the time. But the New Covenant teaches us that we are to define one another by this simple truth: "Christ in you – the hope of glory" (Colossians 1:27). And the heart of Christian community means seeing beyond someone's sin (or giftedness) to seeing what Jesus is doing or what He longs to do in that person (see Galatians 1: 15-16); then helping them see that, and releasing the unique manifestation of Christ-in-them.

Sermon

[Note: Prior to the service beginning, you will need to "scope out" the adults that are sitting close by, for you will need to find two or three that will be okay with you picking on them. Try to find folks with some "interesting qualities" – e.g. very tall, long beard, large nose, etc. Again, these will need to be folks won't be shy or offended; and if they are "hams," all the better!]

Begin by looking out at all the children, and then at all the congregation for five or ten seconds. *"Excuse me . . . I'm just trying to get a measure on our congregation – to see what they're like. In fact, I'd like to measure a few of you to get a better idea of who we are . . . ."* [At this point, pull your tape measure from your hip.] Start by quickly measuring some of the kids – getting their height. As you do this, take out your pen and legal pad, and begin recording your findings. For example, *"Wow – Jimmy here is three feet, seven inches! I'll give you ten points for that! (Write this on pad.) And you're wearing a blue shirt! You know, blue is my favorite color! So I'll give you five extra bonus points for that! That gives you a grand total of fifteen points!"* Do similarly for another child or two.

Now start measuring some adults. First I picked on "Russ," who's extremely tall (Everybody laughed when I had Russ stand up; he even commented, "I knew this was coming!) *"Russ, let me measure you . . . Wow! Six feet, eight inches! I'll give you thirty points for that! But you have red hair – minus twenty points!"* (The congregation broke out in laughter – but they were beginning to see my point.) I also picked on "Dave," who had a long beard. *"Dave, let me measure your beard . . . three inches long! Wow! I'll give you forty points for that! Now, lift up your arm, please.* (I gestured like I was going to measure his arm, but it was a ruse. What I then did was smell his armpit.) *Minus 50!"* (Again, the congregation broke out in laughter.) Then I moved to "Vin," who had a good-sized nose. *"Vin, let me measure that honker of yours. . . . Wow! One and one-quarter inches! Thirty five points!"* But again, this was a set-up, as the length of my own nose is legendary; and everyone knew this was coming. *"But Vin, check this out."* (I then measured my nose.) *"Two inches long! One hundred points!"* Then I tallied up all the points, and read the results out loud: *"Fifteen points, twenty five points, thirty points, minus ten points, and one hundred points for me . . . I win!* [It was at this precise point, in a totally spontaneous manner, that Vin shouted out, "By a nose!" The congregation burst out in laughter – and I was laughing so hard I had a hard time recovering!]

I then talked to the children. *Now, let me ask you: Do you think this is how God measures people when He looks at us?* (They all cried out, "NO!") *Well then, what do you think God looks at when He looks at us – how does He see us?* It was amazing: At each of our three services, the kids said something to the effect of, "He looks at our heart." *Yes, when God looks at us, He doesn't measure us according to how big we are or what we look like or how we dress, but God looks at the heart. And if we believe in Jesus, do you know what God sees when He looks at us? He sees Jesus! And Jesus is bigger and more beautiful and more perfect than anyone! That's what He sees! Doesn't that make you feel good?*

Prayer

Lord, thank You that when You look at us, You see Jesus. Forgive us, Lord, for measuring people according to our own rules that we make up. Help us to see people the way *You* do, Lord. Amen.

Thanksgiving
Five Kernels of Corn

Scripture

Acts 4:32-33

"Now the multitude of those who believed were of one heart and one soul; neither did anyone say that any of the things he possessed was his own, but they had all things in common. And with great power the apostles gave witness to the resurrection of the Lord Jesus. And great grace was upon them all."

1 Timothy 6:17-19

"Command those who are rich in this present age not to be haughty, nor to trust in uncertain riches but in the living God, who gives us richly all things to enjoy. Let them do good, that they be rich in good works, ready to give, willing to share, storing up for themselves a good foundation for the time to come, that they may lay hold on eternal life."

Galatians 6:7-9

"Do not be deceived, God is not mocked; for whatever a man sows, that he will also reap. For he who sows to his flesh will of the flesh reap corruption, but he who sows to the Spirit will of the Spirit reap everlasting life. And let us not grow weary while doing good, for in due season we shall reap if we do not lose heart."

cf. Luke 12:16-23

Materials

Five kernels of corn (or more if you intend to share with the children.)

Big Idea

Hoarding excludes others; feasting and celebration requires trust, but invites others in.

Overview

The story of the first Thanksgiving is recorded in the book, *The Light and the Glory*, by Peter Marshall. It is an incredible story of the pilgrims' willingness to risk their storehouse of winter food for the sake of something bigger than themselves: fellowship and feasting with the Wampanoag Indians. God was with them during a very harsh winter that followed, and rewarded their sacrifice and trust by preserving each one of them with very little on which to live. We are similarly faced with such decisions all the time: to hoard what we see as "ours" (whether it be possessions, money, time, energy, or even our very presence), or to give it away, trusting in the goodness of God no matter what the outcome. It really comes down to what we believe about His *goodness*. True "Thanksgiving" is not so much about being thankful for all the "stuff" we have, but being thankful that we have a God who is good and trustworthy enough for us to give it all away.

Sermon

How many of you know when the first Thanksgiving occurred? It occurred in 1621 – in what we now call Massachusetts. The Pilgrims were filled with gratitude, because of their good relationship with Squanto and the Wampanoag Indians. So, Governor Bradford ordered a day of Public Thanksgiving. He invited Massasoit; and to the Pilgrims' surprise Massasoit arrived with ninety Indians – a day early! The Pilgrims didn't expect so many; and they were concerned that if they fed so many people, it would cut into their food supply to get them through the cold winter. So they prayed hard, and they had a choice: to turn the Indians away, or to trust God with what they had and go ahead and have the feast (kind of reminds you of the story of the boy who had five loaves and two fish – and there were over 5,000 people to feed; but Jesus didn't turn them away – He fed them) Do you know what the Pilgrims did? They went ahead and decided to feast and celebrate! And it was an incredible celebration! And they soon discovered that the Indians hadn't come empty-handed; they had brought five deer and a dozen wild turkeys! And they also showed the Pilgrims an Indian delicacy – how to roast kernels of corn in a pot until they popped – all fluffy and white. You know what that is, don't you? ☺

The Pilgrims provided the vegetables – carrots, turnips, cucumbers, beets, cabbage; and they introduced the Indians to blueberry, cherry, and apple pie! Between meals, they all competed in games, contests, races, and wrestling matches. They were having so much fun they extended it to three days! But do you know what happened that winter? It was an extremely cold and harsh winter, and the Pilgrims' food supply ran low – so at one point, they had to ration the food so that each person could only eat five kernels of corn each day. It's hard to imagine they could live on this. But they had a choice once again: they could become bitter toward God and toward the Indians – or even themselves (perhaps feeling foolish) for using up all that food on Thanksgiving. Or, they could choose not to become bittered, and trust Jesus more deeply than they ever had.

Do you know what they did? The chose to trust Jesus – and they lived on five kernels of corn each day (hand out five kernels of corn to each child if possible) . . . and not one of them died that winter. They chose to trust Jesus and believe in His goodness toward them, even though it involved great sacrifice. They chose to continue in joy – rather than to experience regret and bitterness for their generous hearts. For when you close your heart toward others, you will become bitter.

Prayer

Lord, help us to trust in Your goodness toward us – and Your generous heart toward us; so that we might not hold on and grasp what You give us. Help us to have generous hearts toward others with what You've given us – so that we might receive Your joy all of our days. Remind us of Your generosity as we feast this Thanksgiving. Amen.

The Law Kills

Scripture

Galatians 3:24
"Therefore the law was our tutor
that brings us to Christ."

2 Corinthians 3:6
"For the letter kills, but the Spirit gives life."

Big Idea

The Law is a guide that
brings us to Christ.

Materials

None needed.

Overview

Several years ago I preached an adult sermon entitled *"Just Say Yes"* – which was an obvious play on words on the then-popular saying, *"Just Say No" (to drugs)*. The basic idea was from Paul's struggle in Romans 7, that the presence of the law seems to actually increase my desire to disobey it. A verse in Colossians 1 (one of the primary New Covenant passages in the New Testament) caught my attention by its paradoxical truth: "To this end (i.e. to present every man perfect in Christ) I also labor, striving according to His working which works in me mightily." Somehow, there's a difference between striving according to the flesh (like Paul was in Romans 7) and striving according to *His working in me*. This is the essence of the New Covenant of grace. The law was not intended to be fulfilled in us, but to drive us to Christ – who fulfills it through us as we yield to *His* working in us.

Sermon

As the children come up, start shouting at them the words below. The key to this lies in your enthusiasm – you'll need to be frenzied and passionate as you shout at them. Note: You'll need to do it in a way that seems somewhat serious, yet in a way that they know you're not really angry at them – i.e. in a way that they can see the twinkle in your eye. You can do something like this if you've been around awhile and the kids *know you* . . . but don't do this kind of sermon (i.e. where you're yelling at them) if they don't know you and know that you can be silly at times.

Hey – why are all of you sitting on the carpet? Don't you know there's a rule that says that you can't sit on the carpet in church? Come on! What's wrong! Haven't you heard about this rule? How could you not know this! Come on – get up! Everybody up off the carpet!

Now look around at all the kids – look aghast. *Hey, wait a minute! A lot of you are wearing the color blue. Don't you know that we have a law here in church that says that anyone wearing blue can't stand up in the church? Come on! All of you who are wearing blue, you need to sit down! No people with blue can stand in the church!*

Just as they begin to sit down, get on them again: *"Hey – wait a minute! Why are you sitting down?! Don't you remember the first rule – no sitting on the church carpet! Come on! Get with it! Stand up! Hey wait a minute – you're wearing blue! You can't stand up!*

You can augment this if you like, by adding something like white socks, or whatever, but two potentially conflicting rules seems like enough.

At this point, stop talking, lean back, and flash them a big smile. *"Now, let me ask you: how do you feel?"* [One child responded, without hesitation, "Accused!" Others responded with words like "Bad" or "Sad."] *When you're under a lot of laws like this, what do you really long for most? What do you need?* [At this point, one child yelled out, "FREEDOM!" The whole place broke out laughing, for it had evoked the scene from the movie "Braveheart.") *Yeah – you want freedom!*

Now, laws like these are kind of silly – I just made them up. But God gives us laws in the world that are good laws – laws that are meant to be obeyed. But often, it seems like the more we try to obey them, the more we fail. Do you know why God gave so many laws in the Bible? To make us long for grace – to make us long for Jesus! The Bible says in Galations 3 that the Law was like a guide to drive us to Jesus.

Prayer

Lord, thank You so much for giving us Jesus! For it seems the more we try to obey You, the more we fail. So thank You for coming to us and filling us with Your Spirit – for coming and living inside us . . . so that we can receive Your grace and do Your will as You work in us. Amen.

The Sometimes Bitter Taste of Love

Scripture

Hebrews 12:11
"Now no discipline seems to be joyful for the present, but painful; nevertheless, afterward it yields the peaceable fruit of righteousness to those who have been trained by it."

Psalm 107:1
"Give thanks to the Lord, for He is good! For His love endures forever."

Big Idea

A loving Father sometimes does or allows things to His children that feel or seem unloving – which requires their trust in His love.

Materials

A photo of your cat (or other pet), bottle of medicine, syringe.

Overview

Perhaps one of the most painful things for a parent is to have his/her children doubt his/her love. Oftentimes love demands that we do things for the good of our children that might not "feel" or "appear" loving at first glance – but it's done with the good of the child in mind. Asking our children to submit to painful and unpleasant circumstances at the risk of appearing unloving is a painful thing to do – yet perhaps one of the most loving things a parent can do. He risks his own reputation for the sake of love. And He longs for the child to trust in His love – even though the child might not feel it or understand. Such "ruthless trust" (as Brennan Manning calls it) is precious to the heart of any parent – and to God.

Sermon

Do any of you have pets? We have four pets – two cats and two dogs. I'd like to introduce you to one of our cats – his name is Twinkle (put picture of Twinkle up on the screen.) We purchased Twinkle about ten years ago – isn't he beautiful? We paid good money for Twinkle – he belongs to us. But do you know what I do sometimes? Sometimes I chase Twinkle around the house . . . and he's very hard to catch, so I need to trick him by shaking the canister of cat treats . . . and when he comes close, I grab him! And then I take a big, heavy blanket, and I wrap Twinkle in it – round and round – until he's completely bound up so he can't move - with only his head sticking out! And then, with one hand, I pry open his mouth, and then I make him take this medicine. . . . [Show it to the kids – let them smell it.] How does it smell? Yes – it's disgusting! And so with one hand I pry open his mouth, and then with the other hand, I stick this syringe in his mouth and squirt in the medicine! And do you know what happens next?

He throws a hissy-fit!!! He hates that medicine! And he hisses . . . and he scratches . . . and he starts flailing all about and he finally manages to get out of the blanket . . . then he looks at me and hisses some more . . . and then runs away!

Now, here's my question: Am I a loving pet owner? [Most of the children said, "No!" but a few said "Yes." I asked them why they said "Yes," to which they responded, "Because you were trying to help him and give him medicine."]

So, what I hear you saying is that just because I did something that didn't "feel" good or "feel" loving to "Twinkle," that doesn't necessarily mean I don't love Twinkle, does it? Hmmmm . . . that's interesting . . . let's pray!

Prayer

Father, help us to never doubt Your love – even when it seems like You're not there or not loving. Help us to believe in Your goodness and trust in Your loving presence in our lives. Amen.

The Weight of Unforgiveness

Scripture

Mark 11:25-26

"And whenever you stand praying, if you have anything against anyone, forgive him, that your Father in heaven may also forgive you your trespasses. But if you do not forgive, neither will your Father in heaven forgive your trespasses."

Ephesians 4:32

"And be kind to one another, tenderhearted, forgiving one another, even as God in Christ forgave you."

Big Idea

Unforgiveness is like a heavy load on your soul, which keeps you bound up and enslaved to bitterness.

Materials

Knapsack, backpack, or bag of large, heavy rocks.

Overview

I once heard someone describe a healthy soul as having an energy or posture that is "upward and outward." Conversely, they described an unhealthy soul as having an energy or posture in life that is "downward and inward" – bent over, curved in on itself. The Bible even describes such an unhealthy posture as being "bent" – almost like animals – rather than erect and upright, looking up to our heavenly Father (see Psalm 145:14; Psalm 24:7; Jeremiah 2:27). When we are in a state of unforgiveness, it's like we are carrying a large weight on our shoulders which bends us over, binding us up and preventing us from freely looking upward and outward in worship and love. We're bound and bent over in bitterness and resentment. Jesus came to free us by forgiving us – thereby enabling us to forgive and love one another (we no longer have to "cover ourselves" – for He's got us covered!).

Sermon

[Walk in with a very heavy backpack or bag of large rocks over your shoulder; hunched over and obviously laboring in pain.] *Oh! . . . Ugh! . . . Oh! . . . this weight is just about killing me . . . I feel so bent over . . . I feel so weighed down . . . I feel so burdened . . . what can I do? Somebody – please help me and tell me what I can do to get rid of this burden! Please!* [At this point, several of the children yelled out, "Let it go!" So I dropped the bag of rocks onto the stage, making quite a loud thump. At this point, I then paused, looked up, and with a loud shout (reminiscent of Mel Gibson in "Braveheart") yelled out] *FREEDOM!!!!!! I'm free! The burden is gone! You know what that bag of rocks reminds me of? Unforgiveness. For when we don't forgive someone for the hurt they've done to us, we end up carrying a burden which actually hurts **us**, and bends us over and binds us. Have you ever had someone hurt you or sin against you? God wants us to forgive them – because if we don't, it's like placing a heavy burden on our shoulders. And what's worse, we won't be like Jesus – who has a heart that always longs to forgive.*

Prayer

Lord, forgiveness is a hard thing. Help us to trust You when we're sinned against – so that we might entrust our hurt to You, so that we might be like You and forgive – so that we might be free to love. In Your name, Amen.

The Wind Blows Where it Wills

Scripture

Genesis 2:7
"And the Lord God formed man of the dust of the ground, and breathed into his nostrils the breath of life; and man became a living being."

John 3:8
"The wind blows where it wishes, and you hear the sound of it, but cannot tell where it comes from and where it goes. So is everyone who is born of the Spirit."

Acts 2:2,4
"And suddenly there came a sound from heaven, as of a rushing, mighty wind, and it filled the whole house where they were sitting . . . and they were all filled with the Holy Spirit. . . ."

Big Idea

Some of the best things in life are not seen, but experienced.

Materials

Small fan, extension cord, confetti (or small pieces of paper).

Overview

I once heard Eugene Peterson teach that the work of the Spirit is a story of three movements: The Spirit is seen in Creation, Salvation, and Holy Living (ref. above verses) Of the three members of the Trinity, the Holy Spirit is often most mysterious and least understood, often thought of as a ghost or some wispy, vague life force. How to understand this member of the Godhead who is described in the Bible as "wind"? And more to the point: how do we perceive and engage with something that we cannot see? (*"No one has seen God at any time"* – John 1:18). Is that what defines the reality of its existence? Often, in our modernist thinking, we reason that if something can't be seen, it's not worth engaging. Yet the Scriptures are replete with the basic truth that some of the best things in life are not seen, but *experienced*. As Jesus said to a doubting Thomas, "Blessed are those who don't see, and yet believe."

Sermon

*I've got a problem, and I wanted to see if you can help me out. We all be-
lieve in God, right? You believe in Him – yet how many of you have seen
Him? Have you ever seen Him? Maybe a few of you have, but I haven't yet
seen Him with my eyes. So if I haven't actually seen Him with my eyes,
how do I know He exists? How do I know He's for real?*

*Well, let me ask you: Have any of you ever seen the wind? (No.) How
do you know the wind is for real if you can't see it? You know it's real because you can see what the wind does to things – like trees, and clouds,
and leaves. Let's take a look at this* (turn on fan). *Can you see the wind?*
(No!) *Now, drop pieces of paper in front of the fan. Can you see the
wind now? Yes – you can see what the wind is doing to the paper – it's
moving it along. It's the same way with God! We might not be able to always see Him, but we can sure see what He does to people – giving us
peace, giving us strength in hard times, changing our hearts that are hard
and making them soft. (I think that's the greatest evidence that God is really
real!)*

Prayer

Lord, help us to remember that some of the best things in life aren't
seen, but are experienced. Lord, we don't often see You with our eyes,
but we sure do experience our presence in our lives. Thank You that
You're real – more real than anything on this earth. Increase our faith
to believe in You. Amen.

Trinitarian Play

Scripture

John 1:18
"No one has seen God at any time. The only begotten Son, who is in the bosom of the Father, He has declared Him."

John 15:26
"But when the Helper comes, whom I shall send to you from the Father, the Spirit of truth who proceeds from the Father, He will testify of Me."

Matthew 28:19
"Go therefore and make disciples of all nations, baptizing them in the name of the Father, and of the Son, and of the Holy Spirit. . . ."

Big Idea

The Trinity is somewhat like a play, where you have the playwright (Father), the Script (Son), and the Director (Holy Spirit).

Materials

Notebook, pen.

Overview

The Trinity is a difficult concept to grasp, even for adults. But sometimes, in their childlike innocence, children tend to grasp difficult concepts that we adults struggle with. They see the simplicity of it, while we focus on the complexity. I knew that this children's sermon would be "pushing the edge" for such young minds. But I wanted to give it a shot, and I was amazed to find that many of the kids did grasp the analogy – or at least parts of it. This sermon was inspired by my reading of Dorothy Sayers' classic book, *The Mind of the Maker*. This book may be the best work I have ever come across which attempts to tackle difficult concepts like the Trinity, Divine sovereignty, and human responsibility. Sayers uses the analogy of a "play" to illuminate the unique facets of the three members of the Trinity. To have a play you first need an "idea" or a "story" – which begins in the mind of the playwright. You can't see it (like you can't see God the Father) – but the story is there. The next step for the playwright is to take what is in his mind and make it incarnate – i.e. to write it down on paper – into a script – for all to see. This of course is analogous to the Incarnate Son. Then, once you have a script, you need a director who will take that script and guide the actors and actresses who need to get the script inside of them. This of course is akin to the work of the Holy Spirit. The amazing thing is that the playwright receives great joy as He watches the characters take His script and "play it out" according to their own interpretation and uniqueness. Yet they do follow a script that has come from the mind of the playwright.

Sermon

How many of you have ever been to a play? OK – if you're going to have a play, what do you need? [Most of the kids said "props, costumes, and actors."] *Yes, you need all these things, but what's the most important thing you need in order to have a play? You need a story! Now, where does a story for a play come from?* [One child yelled out, "From God!"] *The story comes from the person who thinks up the play, right? He or she is called the "playwright." Now, say the playwright thinks up a story in his or her head. Can you see it? No! So the playwright now needs to somehow take the story that's in his head, and he needs to do what?* [The kids were tracking here – as they yelled out, "Write it down!"] *Yes! The playwright needs to write it down* [Take out notepad and begin writing on it.] *This is called the "script." Now, once you have the script, what needs to happen next? Yes! You need actors and actresses who will look at the script and memorize it and get it inside them, and then you need a director who will help them to interpret the script and to know how to act out their parts.*

We worship one God, right? But we worship the Father, Son, and Holy Spirit, right? This is called the Trinity. So, does that mean we worship three Gods? [Nearly all the kids said "No!" – which was a testament to our children's department!] *No – we worship one God – who exists in three persons. This is pretty hard to understand, isn't it? But I was thinking that when you want to understand the Trinity, think about a play. Because in order to have a play, you need a playwright who has a story in his head; so you can't see the story – but you know it's there. That's kind of like the Father. Then you need to have the playwright write out the story that's in his head – to "incarnate" it onto some paper so you can see it. That's kind of like Jesus – who reveals the Father. Then you need a director to help the actors interpret the script and act it out correctly – that's kind of like the Holy Spirit – who helps the script to get inside us! Let's pray.*

Prayer

Lord, thanks for revealing Your story to us. Thank You for Jesus. And thank You for the presence of the Holy Spirit in our lives. And thank You for letting us live out Your story – each of us in our own unique way. Amen.

St. Valentine's Day

Scripture

1 John 4:16-18a

"And we have known and believed the love that God has for us. God is love, and he who abides in love abides in God, and God in him. Love has been perfected among us in this: that we may have boldness in the Day of Judgment; because as He is, so are we in this world. There is no fear in love; but perfect love casts out fear."

2 Timothy 1:7

"For God has not given us a spirit of fear, but of power and of love and of a sound mind."

Song of Solomon 8:6

"Set me as a seal upon your heart, as a seal upon your arm; for love is as strong as death, jealousy as severe as the grave; Its flames are flames of fire; a most vehement flame."

Big Idea

Love overcomes fear and is as strong as death.

Materials

None needed. [Optional: dress in character from this period.]

Overview

This children's sermon is a bit different from most, in that it is more of a dramatic presentation, rather than an object lesson invoking questions and dialogue. It is a dramatic narrative regarding the story of St. Valentine, who lived in the 3rd century in Rome. There is debate about his story, and differing versions and interpretations, but this story seems to be one of the more common ones regarding the meaning behind the holiday which bears his name. The story is a testament to the power of love.

Sermon

Let me introduce myself. My name is Valentine. I lived in Rome during the third century. That was long, long ago! At that time, Rome was ruled by an emperor named Claudius. I didn't like Emperor Claudius, and I wasn't the only one! A lot of people shared my feelings.

Claudius wanted to have a big army. He expected men to volunteer to join. Many men just did not want to fight in wars. They did not want to leave their wives and families. As you might have guessed, not many men signed up. This made Claudius furious. So what happened? He had a crazy idea. He thought that if men were not married, they would not mind joining the army. So Claudius decided not to allow any more marriages. Young people thought his new law was cruel. I thought it was preposterous! I certainly wasn't going to support that law!

Did I mention that I was a priest? One of my favorite activities was to marry couples. Even after Emperor Claudius passed his law, I kept on performing marriage ceremonies – secretly, of course. It was really quite exciting. Imagine a small candlelit room with only the bride and groom and myself. We would whisper the words of the ceremony, listening all the while for the steps of soldiers.

One night, we did hear footsteps. It was scary! Thank goodness the couple I was marrying escaped in time. I was caught. (Not quite as light on my feet as I used to be, I guess.) I was thrown in jail and told that my punishment was death.

I tried to stay cheerful. And do you know what? Wonderful things happened. Many young people came to the jail to visit me. They threw flowers and notes up to my window. They wanted me to know that they, too, believed in love.

One of these young people was the daughter of the prison guard. Her father allowed her to visit me in the cell. Sometimes we would sit and talk for hours. She helped me to keep my spirits up. She agreed that I did the right thing by ignoring the Emperor and going ahead with the secret marriages. On the day I was to die, I left my friend a little note thanking her for her friendship and loyalty. I signed it, "Love from your Valentine."

I believe that note started the custom of exchanging love messages on Valentine's Day. It was written on the day I died, February 14, 269 A.D. Now, every year on this day, people remember. But most importantly, they think about love and friendship. And when they think of Emperor Claudius, they remember how he tried to stand in the way of love, and they laugh – because they know that love can't be beaten!

Prayer

[I skipped the prayer, given this was a dramatic presentation – but you could add a prayer thanking God for being the original lover and the originator of both divine and human love.]

Voiceless

Scripture

1 Corinthians 12:21
"And the eye cannot say to the hand,
'I have no need of you.'"

1 Corinthians 12:26
"when one member suffers, all the
members suffer with it."

Big Idea

We need each other,
and when one member
of the body suffers,
all suffer with it.

Materials

Cue cards, which someone else will read for you (see below.)

Overview

This children's sermon came about during a bout with laryngitis, during which
I had totally lost my voice. During that week, I came to realize how dependent
I was on my voice, and how difficult life had become without it (this really
came into focus when I pulled up to the McDonald's Drive-thru, the attendant
asked me for my order, and I suddenly remembered that I had no voice with
which to order!). It was then that the idea of this children's sermon came to
me. The fact that I had truly lost my voice gave this sermon its power.

Sermon

Write out each of the following sentences on a cue card. Find someone (e.g. another pastor or recognized leader) to read the cue cards. Hold the cue cards in front of you, and go through them as the other person reads them for you as you flip through them.

Here are the cue cards I used:

Good Morning!

This week I got a cold and I lost my voice!

So I can't talk to you.

And over the past few days I've learned an important lesson.

I learned how important one small part of my body is to the rest of my body.

Do you know what it's like to lose your voice?

On Friday, I was hungry so I drove up to the drive-thru at McDonald's.

And the man in the speaker said, "Can I take your order please?"

And then I remembered, "I can't talk!"

And if you can't talk, you can't order your food.

And if you can't order your food, you can't eat!

And over the past few days people have called me on the phone.

But I couldn't talk with them!

Yikes!

This has reminded me about what the Bible says, that when one part of the body suffers, ALL parts of the body suffer, too!

And when one part of the body suffers, the other parts need to care for that part and love that part.

So that it can get better.

Because we all need each other, and Jesus loves every part.

That's what I learned this week.

Prayer

Let's Pray.
Dear Jesus, thank You for every person in this church.
Help us realize how much we need each other.
Amen!

P.S. Someone told me this morning that if I gargled with apple cider and water, it would help me heal.

YUK!

I guess I'll try it. ☺

Where Do You Bring Your Wounds?

Scripture

James 5:16
"Confess your trespasses to one another, and pray for one another, that you may be healed."

1 John 1:6-7
"If we say we have fellowship with Him, and walk in darkness, we lie and do not practice the truth. But if we walk in the light as He is in the light, we have fellowship with one another, and the blood of Jesus Christ His Son cleanses us from all sin. If we say that we have no sin, we deceive ourselves, and the truth is not in us."

Galatians 6:1-2
"Brethren, if a man is overtaken in any trespass, you who are spiritual restore such a one in a spirit of gentleness, considering yourself lest you also be tempted. Bear one another's burdens, and so fulfill the law of Christ."

Materials

None needed (unless you want to pretend to have an outward wound, in which case you could use some bandages or gauze or an ace bandage).

Big Idea

When we hide our sins and weaknesses from each other, we hurt our fellowship with each other; and the church ceases to be the church, and we remain in darkness.

Overview

I've come to see that the core of the spiritual battle about sin is not so much about the struggle to *not* sin; but more about what we do *after* we sin. All of us sin. God "knows our frame" and "pities us as a father pities his children" (Psalm 103:13-14) The fact that we, fallen people, will sin in this fallen world is a given. But God yearns to show us His grace and kindness, so that we would not shirk back in fear and hiding, as Adam and Eve did when they hid in the bushes after they sinned. The cry of the Father as He "walked in the garden in the cool of the day," yearning for fellowship, is heartbreaking and echoes to this day: "Adam, where *are* you?" The church is to be a "safe place" to be honest about our sin, so that "unfruitful works of darkness" might be exposed and brought into the light (cf. Ephesians 5: 11-14) Yet oftentimes we miss the very point of the church when we cover and hide our sins in the midst of our community, out of fear or pride. Such hiding produces a "split" in our personality and we become "dualistic" in our thinking and living, showing one thing on the outside when in reality we are quite another inside. This leads to a lack of integrity in our souls. To have integrity is to be "integrated" – where our outside matches our inside. But when we hide our sin in fear and shame, we become "dis-integrated" and "segregated" in our very person, and it harms the Body. Looking at 1 John 1:6-7 again recently, I was struck by the fact that when John says "If we say that we have no sin we deceive ourselves, and the truth is not in is," I am not so sure that he's referring to a person who truly believes he *possesses* no sin (although that certainly could be the case) What strikes me is how John says, "If we *say* we have no sin" – i.e. we *know* we have sin – and yet we hide it and don't confess it to one another. Thus we remain in darkness, and are not healed. And it *hurts our fellowship*, for, as John says, "If we walk in the light . . . we have fellowship with one another."

Sermon

[Walk out with some kind of wound. Perhaps a hand that's bandaged up, or perhaps an arm in a sling, or some other kind of obvious wound. For me, I had thrown my back out a few days earlier, so I came out bent over, moaning and groaning about the pain in my back.] *Oh . . . my aching back! I may need to cut short our children's sermon because my back is killing me! Can you guys help me? Can any of you tell me what I should do? My back has been hurting for a couple of days now . . . can anyone tell me what I should do?* [At this, one little boy yelled out, "You need to exercise!" which drew quite a few laughs from the congregation. Another yelled out, "You need to eat pork!" (I have no idea what prompted him to say that!)] *Maybe there's someone who could help me . . . can anyone think of where I might go to get help for my back?* [At this the children yelled out, "To a doctor!" At this, I began to whine.] *Yeah, but I don't WANT to go to a doctor . . . I'm too embarrassed to go to a doctor . . . what if he finds out that I have this problem . . . I'd be SO embarrassed! And besides, I don't want to bother my doctor – he's so busy . . . I don't want to be a bother to him. And also, if I see him, he might make me better.* [At this, I then stopped my "whining" and asked them this question.] *Now let me ask you: Are those good reasons to not see a doctor? No! Of course not! A doctor is not going to be bothered if you go see him with a wound or a problem – because that's why he's there! And if I say I'm embarrassed to see a doctor to show him my wound, that's ridiculous – because that's why he's there! You know, that reminds me of people in the church sometimes. Sometimes, we have a wound or a sin that's really hurting us and burdening us, but we say things like "I'm too embarrassed to share this sin or weakness with anyone" or "I don't want to bother anyone with my sins and problems." And yet, that is why we're here as a church! We're supposed to bear each other's burdens, aren't we? And we're supposed to confess our sins to one another and pray for one another, aren't we? We can do this because Jesus died for our sins – and He took away our shame – so we CAN do this without being embarrassed or ashamed!*

Prayer

Lord, help us to trust You. Forgive us for living in fear and in shame, for not being honest, and hiding our sins from each other. Help us to confess our sins and our weaknesses to one another, so that we might be Your Church, and so we might be healed! Amen.

Who Defines You?

Scripture

Isaiah 55:8-9
"For My thoughts are not your thoughts, nor are your ways My ways," says the Lord. "For as the heavens are higher than the earth, So are My ways higher than your ways, and My thoughts than your ."

Isaiah 5:20-21
"Woe to those who call evil good, and good evil; who put darkness for light, and light for darkness; who put bitter for sweet, and sweet for bitter! Woe to those who are wise in their own eyes, and prudent in their own sight!"

1 Corinthians 1:20, 27
"Has not God made foolish the wisdom of this world. . . . But God has chosen the foolish things of the world to put to shame the wise. . . ."

John 1:1
"In the beginning was the Word, and the Word was with God, and the Word was God. He was in the beginning with God."

Big Idea

The Bible helps define who we are and gives meaning to our lives.

Materials

Large dictionary.

Overview

I've heard it said, "You live according to what you believe to be true." How we define ourselves and define certain words will greatly impact how we view ourselves and live by these words. The prevailing culture around us is clamoring to provide definition and meaning to how we see ourselves and our lives (e.g. "You deserve a break today," "All I want for my children is that they're happy," "He is a handsome and successful man," etc.). But very often our wisdom is not God's wisdom, and our ways are not His ways. What seems foolish to the world is wisdom in the sight of God, and what seems wise to a man is foolish in the sight of God. We look to Jesus to define us and provide meaning for our lives in a dark and distorted culture.

Sermon

[Hold up a dictionary.] *What is this?* [A dictionary!] *What does it "do"?*
[It tells you what a word means.] *Yes! It defines words for us – it gives
us their meaning. Let's try it out; let's look up a word and see what it means.
What word shall we look up?* [At this point, I had previously instructed
Peter, our senior pastor, to shout out the word "success," before the
kids had the chance to shout out some words.] *What's that? You want
to look up the definition of success? Thank you for that randomly selected
word, Peter!* [This got a lot of laughs from the congregation.] *OK – let's
look up the definition of the word "success" according to the way that most
people in the world have defined it. Hmmm . . .* [The following are actual
definitions from a dictionary]:

- *The gaining of wealth, fame*
- *The prosperous end of anything attempted*
- *Achieving or attaining one's desired end or goal*

*In other words, success is defined as "getting rich and famous, or achiev-
ing what you set out to do." Do you believe that? You know, I was thinking
about Jesus. He preached and taught for three years, but in the end, He
was crucified. Is that a "success"?* [There was a mixed reaction from the
kids – but most said, "No."] *Do you think it was a success from God's
perspective?* [All enthusiastically said, "Yes!"] *Jesus is kind of like a dictionary for us – because He IS the Word of God – and He gives us meaning.
And His definition of things like success is sometimes a lot different from
the way the world defines success. We need to look to Him for meaning in
our lives. Let's pray . . .*

Prayer

Lord, we need You to define who we are. Thank You that You not only
give us meaning – but You ARE the meaning – the very Word of God.
Help us to get our meaning from You. Amen.

Appendix

- The Strategy of the Children's Sermon
- The Role of the Children
- The Role of the Adults
- The Creative Process
- Preparation and Coordination
- The Role of Humor
- The Role of Objects and Props
- The Format

The Strategy of the Children's Sermon in the Corporate Setting

Our church scheduled the children's sermon early in the service, for a variety of practical reasons (not least of which was to give young children a chance to worship for a while with their families, before they left for their own programs). Yet placing the children's sermon up front also serves an important social, emotional, and theological purpose.

When Christians come together corporately to worship, we usually bring a lot of mental baggage and distractions. Thus, our ministry team viewed the first ten minutes or so of the worship service as *reorientation* – a reorienting of our hearts and minds to what is truly most needed in our souls. Bearing that in mind, we chose an opening song that was usually somewhat loud and rousing, jarring us and calling us to set aside our individual concerns and needs for the sake of something bigger and greater: our need to worship God. And the children's sermon played just as big a part in this process. It too was designed to reorient and prepare our hearts for a key theme or thrust that would be developed through the entire service.

The Role of the Children

I have observed that many children's sermons are often just that: "sermons" – monologues, with no room for dialogue.

212

This is unfortunate, because children make the best theologians, having no preconceived categories through which to filter their sense of wonder and curiosity. Giving them an opportunity to speak is at the very core of the children's sermon. Of course, this is admittedly risky, because you never know where a child will lead you! (Recall that totally unexpected response when I asked the difference between mommies and daddies!) Yet this very truth illustrates a crucial difference between New Covenant and Old: one requires relational engagement and trust in the process, while the other requires no engagement and only a little trust.

In this book, I have included some actual responses of children to my questions during the children's sermon. Their responses are often surprising, refreshing, profound, hilarious, innocent, challenging, and even piercing. No wonder Jesus rebuked His disciples when they tried to keep children from coming to Him. Of such is the Kingdom of Heaven!

The Role of the Adults

In the church setting, the children's sermon has a dual audience. If it didn't, there would be no use in making it part of the adult worship service. As the sermon-giver, I'm always very aware that adults are listening, and of how my sermon will contribute to the entire worship experience for them as well as their young ones.

Yet there is a fine line I must walk here. I always have to remember that the children are my primary audience – thus, the language I use and the manner I speak in must always reflect this. I make it a habit to look directly at the children during the sermon, assuring them of my full attention. They need to know *they're* the ones I'm speaking to.

However, at the same time, I'm keenly aware that the adults' hearts are being prepared and softened for what Jesus longs to do in them during the worship experience. The closing prayer is a key component of the process, where I attempt to summarize the sermon in a way that's effective for both the children and the adults.

The Creative Process

The creative process in developing the children's sermon necessarily begins with the posture of my heart and mind. Am I open to creative possibilities, and not limited by preconceived ideas? Am I bound by linear thinking, or can my mind be stretched by paradox?

When I first began doing children's sermons, I found the process excruciatingly difficult. My mind had been trained in seminary to think in "left-brain," linear ways. Fortunately for me, I've had the privilege of being exposed to creative thinkers (my wife first and foremost, along with some wonderful mentors), and to sit under the most creative preaching I could ever hope for. These, more than anything, have helped me in the creative process.

And I have found it to be crucial in my life to exercise my creativity. This isn't much different from exercising in the physical realm; the more we exercise the creative cells of our brain, the easier things tend to come to us. At first, it took me an hour or two of sitting and contemplating before an idea for a children's sermon came to me. Now those creative thoughts come in a matter of minutes. (It took a few years for me to get to this point).

Just as exercise is important for our bodies, we need to exercise to our brains and hearts. That's why I continually try to expose myself to creative speakers, thinkers, writers, musicians, filmmakers, and artists. My interaction with their ideas and works has been invaluable in the development of my own creative process. Also, I try to deliberately expose myself to writers who are "outside my normal circles." Such writers stretch me and require more from me as I read. Along these lines, I also try to occasionally read books which are "above my level." I once had a professor who encouraged us to try to read books that were "one or two levels above you." He said that we would soon realize that we'd eventually become more familiar with the new and strange terminology, and gradually work ourselves up to that level.

Preparation and Coordination

Another factor in why children's sermons have come more easily to me over time is the relationship I developed with our preaching pastor. The more you get to know your preacher and how he or she thinks, the easier it is to coordinate the children's sermon with the adult sermon, and to achieve integration within the overall worship service. (If you're a pastor that does both the adult and children's sermons, then your task is all the easier!)

It took some time, but I learned to discern the fine line needed for letting a children's sermon lead into the adult sermon *without stealing its thunder*. You don't want to reveal the preacher's main point prematurely, or that might deflate any creative "tension" he or she may want to develop in their sermon. Communication and dialogue with the preaching pastor is essential in terms of this preparation.

The Role of Humor

I have deliberately worked hard to *create opportunity* for humor in the children's sermon. I use this particular phrase purposefully, because it's usually the kids who make the children's sermon so hilarious (and even more effective). Yet there is an art to designing the elements of the sermon so that they lend themselves to humorous interaction. It takes time and effort to word a question just right so that it elicits an engaging response. But it's worth that effort, because humor is crucial at this stage in the service.

Keep in mind, children and adults come into a worship service from all kinds of "places" – some having been dragged by their spouse or parents, some having just had a fight in the car, some skeptical about church entirely. The children's sermon, particularly through its humor, can break up fallow ground: it can help adults to relax, as well as galvanize their focus. Of course, humor often can convey deep and piercing truths that wouldn't get through otherwise. As my former seminary professor Howard Hendricks used to say, "Laughter serves the purpose of opening the mouth – into which you can then deposit difficult truth!"

It truly is amazing what a preacher is able to say when people's defenses are lowered by humor – a principle with which every spouse or parent ought to be thoroughly familiar!

The Role of Objects and Props

It's no great secret that children love object lessons. What we ministers often forget, though, is just how effective object lessons are with *adults*. Many times over the years, people said to me, "I can't remember much of the [adult] sermon, but I'll never forget seeing you crush those grapes with your bare feet, and the image of redemptive suffering I've taken with me from that."

I relate this knowing full well that in that church I experienced some of the most creative, gifted preaching I've ever had the privilege to hear. Yet this person's comment just goes to show the power of sensual stimulation – whether it be visual, audio, smell, or touch. Christianity itself is a *sensual* religion: we baptize with water; we pray with the laying-on of hands; we anoint with oil; we meditate with art; we partake of Christ with bread and wine. Indeed, this "tangibility" lies at the heart of the incarnation:

"And the word became flesh and dwelt among us. . . . No one has seen God at any time. The only begotten Son, who is in the bosom of the Father, He has declared Him. . . . That which was from the beginning, which we have heard, which we have seen with our eyes, which we have looked upon, and our hands have handled, concerning the Word of life." (John 1:14, 18; 1 John 1:1).

The Format

The format or structure of a children's sermon begins with the *Big Idea*. This is the beginning point for the entire process of developing the children's sermon. As with any adult sermon, the basic idea of this sermon ought to be reducible to a single sentence. Once this *Big Idea* is determined, the creative process is employed to flesh out the sermon.

I've found it helpful at this *Big Idea* stage to try to think of corresponding *objects* or *experiences common to children*. For example, if the *Big Idea* has to do with the Holy Spirit, I may think of the wind, and choose to use an object such as a fan (see "The Wind" sermon). Or, if the *Big Idea* is the *filling* of the Holy Spirit, I may think of an object that can be filled with something (see the "Chocolate Milk Gospel" sermon).

Sometimes, the *Big Idea* of the children's sermon doesn't correspond to the Big Idea of the adult sermon – but, rather, leads into the *opening* thought or idea of the adults' message. In this way, the children's sermon can serve to "set up" the adult sermon. Of course, sometimes the children's sermon will have little or nothing to do with the adult sermon. Instead, it may tie into a theme that's being developed for the worship service (e.g., a particular song), or serve to highlight special holidays or themes from the church calendar.

With the *Big Idea* determined, I've found that the following elements help to complete the format of the children's sermon. I have provided these in each of the sermons contained in this book:

* Corresponding *Scriptures* are provided, to highlight the biblical concepts that the sermon is intending to convey.

* An *Overview* is offered, to develop and illustrate the New Covenant idea or thinking behind the children's sermon. This can assist in developing a "way of thinking" about the implications of the New Covenant.

* A list of *Materials* is given (including objects or props). Of course these can be adapted for different settings and for when certain resources (such as audio-visual equipment) is not available.

* The actual *Sermon* is then written out. Included in some of the sermons are actual responses by children. These illustrate the importance of structuring the sermon in such a way as to elicit responses and dialogue from the kids – which, of course, brings joy to the sermon when preached.

* A *Closing Prayer* is offered, which serves important purposes. The obvious importance is to offer the entire sermon to God, so that the Holy Spirit might seal the truths discussed in the minds and hearts of both the children and the adults. Yet the closing prayer also serves to recap or summarize the Big Idea, and can help pull it all together particularly for the adults, who will remain in the service.

Resources from Healthy Life Press

We've Got Mail: The New Testament Letters in Modern English – As Relevant Today as Ever! by Rev. Warren C. Biebel, Jr. is a modern English paraphrase of the New Testament Letters, especially designed to inspire in readers a loving appreciation for God's Word. (Printed: $9.95; PDF eBook: $6.95; together: $15.00 at www.healthylifepress.com).

Hearth & Home - Recipes for Life, by Karey Swan (7th Edition) is far more than a cookbook, this classic is a life book, with recipes for life as well as for great food. Karey describes how to buy and prepare from scratch a wide variety of tantalizing dishes, while weaving into the book's fabric the wisdom of the ages plus the recipe that she and her husband used to raise their kids. A great gift for Christmas or for a new bride. Perfect Bound Version (8 x 10, glossy cover): $17.95; PDF eBook version: $12.95; Together as set: $24.95 only at www.healthylifepress.com.

Who Me, Pray? Prayer 101: Praying Aloud, for Beginners, by Gary A. Burlingame (Printed: $6.95 eBook: $2.99 - together $7.95 at www.healthylifepress.com). *Who Me, Pray?* is a practical guide for prayer, based on Jesus' direction in "The Lord's Prayer," with examples provided for use in typical situations where you might be asked or expected to pray in public.

The Big Black Book – What the Christmas Tree Saw, by Rev. Warren C. Biebel, Jr (Printed: $7.95; PDF eBook: $4.95; Together: $10.95 at www.healthylifepress.com). An original Christmas story, from the perspective of the Christmas tree. This little book is especially suitable for parents to read to their children at Christmas time or all year-round.

My Broken Heart Sings, the poetry of Gary Burlingame (Printed: $10.95; PDF eBook: $6.95; Together: $13.95 at www.healthylifepress.com). In 1987, Gary and his wife Debbie lost their son Christopher John, at only six months of age, to a chronic lung disease. This life-changing experience gave them a special heart for helping others through similar loss and pain.

After Normal: One Teen's Journey Following Her Brother's Death, by Diane Aggen. *After Normal* is based on a journal the author kept following the death of her brother. It offers helpful insights and understanding for teens facing a similar loss or for those who might wish to understand and help teens facing a similar loss. (Printed: $11.95; eBook: $6.95; together: $15.00 at www.healthylifepress.com).

In the Unlikely Event of a Water Landing – Lessons Learned from Landing in the Hudson River, by Andrew Jamison, MD. The author was flying standby on US Airways Flight 1549 toward Charlotte on January 15, 2009, from New York City, where he had been inter-viewing for a residency position. Little did he know that the next stop would be the Hudson River. These are lessons learned about the sovereignty of God over all things. Riveting and inspirational, this book would be especially helpful for people in need of hope and encouragement. (Printed: $8.95; PDF eBook: $6.95; Together: $12.95 at www.healthylifepress.com).

Finding Martians in the Dark – Everything I Needed to Know About Teaching Took Me Only 30 Years to Learn, by Dan M. Biebel (Printed: $10.95; PDF eBook: $6.95; Together: $15.00. Packed with wise advice based on hard experience, and laced with humor, this book is perfect for a teacher's gift year-round. Parents with kids in Jr. or Sr. High love it, too. Susan J. Wegmann, PhD, says, "Biebel's sardonic wit is mellowed by a genuine love for kids and teaching. . . . A Whitman-like sensibility flows through his stories of teaching, learning, and life."

Because We're Family and *Because We're Friends*, by Gary A. Burlingame. Sometimes things related to faith can be hard to discuss with your family and friends. These booklets are designed to be given as gifts, to help you open the door to discussing spiritual matters with family members and friends who are open to such a conversation. (Printed: $5.95 each; PDF eBook: $4.95 each; Together: $9.95 per pair (printed & eBook of the same title, at www.healthylifepress.com).

The Transforming Power of Story: How Telling Your Story Brings Hope to Others and Healing to Yourself, by Elaine Leong Eng, MD, and David B. Biebel, DMin (Printed: $14.99; eBook: $9.99; together: $19.99, only at www.healthylifepress.com). This book demonstrates, through multiple true life stories, how sharing one's story, especially in a group setting, can bring hope to listeners and healing to the one who shares. Designed for group use, individuals facing difficulties will find this book greatly encouraging.

You Deserved a Better Father: Good Parenting Takes a Plan, by Robb Brandt, MD., is about parenting by intention, and other lessons the author learned through the loss of his firstborn son. It is especially for parents who believe that bits and pieces of leftover time will be enough for their own children. (Printed: $10.95 each; PDF eBook: $6.95 each; Together: $12.95 (printed & eBook) at www.healthylifepress.com.

eBook Cover

Jonathan, You Left Too Soon, by David B. Biebel, DMin. One pastor's journey through the loss of his son, into the darkness of depression, and back into the light of joy again, emerging with a renewed sense of mission. (Printed: $6.00; eBook: $5.99; Set: $10.00: set available only at www.healthylifepress.com).

Printed Cover

The Spiritual Fitness Checkup for the 50-Something Woman, by Sharon V. King, PhD. Following the stages of a routine medical exam, the author describes ten spiritual fitness "checkups" midlife women can conduct to assess their spiritual health and tone up their relationship with God. Each checkup consists of the author's personal reflections, a Scripture reference for meditation, and a "Spiritual Pulse Check," with exercises readers can use for personal application. (Printed: $8.95; eBook: $6.95; Set: $12.95 - set available at www.healthylifepress.com).

The Other Side of Life - Over 60? God Still Has a Plan for You, by Rev. Warren C. Biebel Jr. Drawing on biblical examples and his 60-plus years of pastoral experience, Rev. Biebel helps older (and younger) adults understand God's view of aging and the rich life available to everyone who seeks a deeper relationship with God as they age. Rev. Biebel explains how to: Identify God's ongoing plan for your life; Rely on faith to manage the anxieties of aging; Form positive, supportive relationships; Cultivate patience; Cope with new technologies; Develop spiritual integrity; Understand the effects of dementia; Develop a Christ-centered perspective of aging. (Printed: $10.95; eBook: $6.95; Set: $15.00 – set available only at www.healthylifepress.com).

My Faith, My Poetry by Gary A. Burlingame. This unique book of Christian poetry is actually two in one. The first collection of poems, *A Day in the Life*, explores a working parent's daily journey of faith. The reader is carried from morning to bedtime, from "In the Details," to "I Forgot to Pray," back to "Home Base," and finally to "Eternal Love Divine." The second collection of poems, *Come Running*, is wonder, joy, and faith wrapped up in words that encourage and inspire the mind and the heart. (Printed: $10.95; PDF eBook: $6.95; Together: $13.95 at www.healthylifepress.com).

Unless otherwise noted on the site itself, shipping is free for all products purchased through www.healthylifepress.com.

On Eagles' Wings, by Sara Eggleston. This is one woman's life journey from idyllic through chaotic to joy, carried all the way by the One who has promised to never leave us nor forsake us. Remarkable, poignant, moving, and inspiring, this autobiographical account will help many who are facing difficulties that seem too great to overcome or even bear at all. It is proof that Isaiah 40:31 is as true today as when it was penned, "But they that wait upon the LORD shall renew their strength; they shall mount up with wings as eagles; they shall run, and not be weary; and they shall walk, and not faint." (Printed: $14.95; eBook: $8.95; Together: $22.95 at www.healthylifepress.com).

Richer Descriptions, by Gary A. Burlingame, is a unique and handy manual, covering all nine human senses in seven chapters, for Christian speakers and writers. Exercises and a speaker's checklist equip speakers to engage their audiences in a richer experience. Writing examples and a writer's guide help writers bring more life to the characters and scenes of their stories. Bible references encourage a deeper appreciation of being created by God for a sensory existence. (Printed: $15.95; eBook: $8.95; Together: $22.95 at www.healthylifepress.com).

ABOUT HEALTHY LIFE PRESS:

HEALTHY LIFE PRESS was founded with a primary goal of helping previously unpublished authors to get their works to market, and to reissue worthy, previously published works that were no longer available. Our mission is to help people toward optimal vitality by providing resources promoting physical, emotional, spiritual, and relational health as viewed from a Christian perspective. We see health as a verb, and achieving optimal health as a process – a crucial process for followers of Christ if we are to love the Lord with all our heart, soul, mind, AND strength, and our neighbors as ourselves – for as long as He leaves us here. We are a collaborative and cooperative small Christian publisher. For information about publishing with us, e-mail us at: healthylifepress@aol.com.

Treasuring Grace, by Rob Plumley and Tracy Roberts. *This novel was inspired by a dream.* Liz Swanson is a loving wife and mother. Her life isn't quite what she'd imagined, but she considers herself lucky. She has a good husband, beautiful children, and fulfillment outside of her home through volunteer work. On some days she doesn't even notice the dull ache in her heart. While she's preparing for their summer kickoff at Lake George, the ache disappears and her sudden happiness is mistaken for anticipation of their weekend. However, as the family heads north, there are clouds on the horizon that have nothing to do with the weather. A careful observer might see the signs that something is wrong, but only Liz's daughter, who's found some of her mother's hidden journals, has any idea. By the end of the weekend, there will be no escaping the truth or its painful buried secrets, and it will take all of their strength to get through the storm together. Printed: $12.95; eBook: $7.95; together: $19.95 at www.healthylifepress.com).

Life's A Symphony, by Mary Z. Smith. When Kate Spence Cooper receives the news that her husband, Jack, has been killed in the war, she and her young son Jeremy move back to Crawford Wood, Tennessee to be closer to family. Since Jack's death Kate feels that she's lost trust in everyone, including God. Will she ever find her way back to the only One whom she can always depend upon? The sleepy little town of Crawford Wood  is a place where families still attend church on a regular basis. It's a place where people reach out to each other with love and compassion. Kate's parents own and operate "Simple Pleasures," an antique store situated in the center of town. Will Kate accept the job they offer her? And what about Kate's match making brother, Chance? The cheeky man has other ideas on how to bring happiness into his sister's life once more. (Printed: $12.95; PDF eBook: $7.95; together: $19.95 at www.healthylifepress.com).

From Orphan to Physician – The Winding Path, by Chun-Wai Chan, MD. "In this book, Dr. Chan describes how his family escaped to Hong Kong, how they survived in utter poverty, and how he went from being an orphan to graduating from Harvard Medical School and becoming a cardiologist. The writing is fluent, easy to read and understand. The sequence of events is realistic, emotionally moving, spiritually touching, heart-warming, and thought provoking. The book illustrates . . . how one must have faith in order to walk through life's winding path." – Excerpted from the Foreword by Rev. Peter Lai (Printed: $14.95; eBook: $8.95; Together: $22.95, set available only at www.healthylifepress.com).

12 Parables, by Wayne Faust. Timeless Christian stories about the things we all face in our spiritual walk – doubt, fear, change, grief, and more. Using tight, entertaining prose, professional musician and comedy performer Wayne Faust manages to deal with difficult concepts in a simple, straightforward way. These are stories you can read aloud over and over – to your spouse, your family, or in a group setting. Packed with emotion and just  enough mystery to keep you wondering, while providing lots of points to ponder and discuss when you're through, these stories relate the gospel in the tradition of the greatest speaker of parables the world has ever known, who appears in them often. (Printed: $14.95; eBook: $8.95; Together: $22.95, set available only at www.healthylifepress.com).

Pieces of My Heart, by David L. Wood. Eighty-two lessons from normal everyday life. David's hope is that that these stories will spark thoughts about God's constant involvement and intervention in our lives and stir a sense of how much He cares about every detail that is important to us. The piece missing represents his son, Daniel, who died in a fire shortly before his first birthday. (374 pages; Printed: $16.95; eBook: $8.95; Set: $24.95 at www.healthylifepress.com).

The Answer is Always "Jesus," by Aram Haroutunian, who gave children's sermons for 15 years at a large church in Golden, Colorado – well over 500 in all. This book contains 74 of his most unforgettable presentations – due to the children's responses. Pastors, homeschoolers, parents who often lead family devotions, or other storytellers will find these stories, along with comments about props and how to prepare and present them, an invaluable asset in reconnecting with the simplest, most profound truths of Scripture, and then to envision how best to communicate these so even a child can understand them.(Printed: $12.95; eBook: $8.95; Together: $19.95, set available only at www.healthylifepress.com).

Handbook of Faith by Rev. Warren C. Biebel Jr. The *New York Times World 2011 Almanac* claims that there are two billion, two hundred thousand Christians in the world, with "Christians" being defined as "followers of Christ." The original twelve followers of Christ changed the world; indeed, they changed the history of the world. So this author, a pastor with over sixty years' experience, poses and answers this logical question: "If there are so

many 'Christians' on this planet, why are they so relatively ineffective in serving the One they claim to follow?" Answer: Because, unlike Him, they do not know and trust the Scriptures, implicitly. This little volume will help you do that. (Printed: $8.95; eBook: $6.95; Together: $13.95, set available only at www.healthylifepress.com).

Dream House by Justa Carpenter. Written by a New England builder of several hundred homes, the idea for this book came to him one day as he was driving that came to him one day as was driving from one jobsite to another. He pulled over and recorded it so he would remember it, and now you will remember it, too, if you believe, as he does, that ". . . He who has begun a good work in you will complete it until the day of Jesus Christ." (Printed: ▨▨▨.95; eBook: $▨.95; Set: $1▨.95 (set only at www.healthylifepress.com).

RECOMMENDED RESOURCES

PRO-LIFE DVD SERIES:
SEE WWW.HEALTHYLIFEPRESS.COM (SELECT "DVD")
FOR TRAILERS AND SPECIAL COMBINATION PRICING

Actual ultrasound image

EYEWITNESS 2 (PUBLIC SCHOOL VERSION)
This DVD has been used in many public schools. It is a fascinating journey through 38 weeks of pregnancy, showing developing babies via cutting edge digital ultrasound technology. Separate chapters allow viewing distinct segments individually. List Price: $34.95; Sale Price: $24.95.

WINDOW TO THE WOMB (2 DVD DISC SET)
Disc 1: Ian Donald (1910-1987) "A Prophetic Legacy;" Disc 2: "A Journey from Death To Life" (50 min). Includes history of sonography and its increasing impact against abortion – more than 80% of expectant parents who "see" their developing baby choose for life. Perfect for counseling and education in Pregnancy Centers, Christian schools, homeschools, and churches. List: $49.95; Sale: $34.95.

WINDOW TO THE WOMB
(PREGNANCY CARE & COUNSELING VERSION)
Facts about fetal development, abortion complications, post-abortion syndrome, and healing. Separate chapters allow selection of specialized presentations to accommodate the needs and time constraints of their situations. List: $34.95; Sale: $24.95.

Unless otherwise noted on our company website itself, shipping is free for all products purchased through www.healthylifepress.com.

If God Is So Good, Why Do I Hurt So Bad?, by David B. Biebel, DMin. In this best-selling classic (nearly 200,000 copies in print worldwide, in five languages) on the subject of loss and renewal, first published in 1989, the author comes alongside people in pain, and shows the way through and beyond it, to joy again. This book has proven helpful to those who are struggling and to those who wish to understand and help. Revised and re-released July 2010. (Printed: $12.95; eBook: $8.95; Set: $19.95 at www.healthylifepress.com).

52 Ways to Feel Great Today, by David B. Biebel, DMin, James E. Dill, MD, and Bobbie Dill, RN. Originally published with the title *50 Ways to Feel Great Today*, this book was revised, updated, and re-released by Florida Hospital Publishing in late 2011. New table of contents, practical tips following each chapter, and two totally new chapters. Available at www.Amazon.com, or visit: http://www.floridahospitalpublishing.com/shop.

OTHER COMING TITLES BY HEALTHY LIFE PRESS

A Simply Homemade Clean, by homesteader Lisa Barthuly. "Somewhere along the path, it seems we've lost our gumption, the desire to make things ourselves," says the author. "Gone are the days of 'do it yourself.' Really . . . why bother? There are a slew of retailers just waiting for us with anything and everything we could need; packaged up all pretty, with no thought or effort required. It is the manifestation of 'progress' . . . right?" I don't buy that!" Instead, Lisa describes how to make safe and effective cleansers for home, laundry, and body right in your own home. This saves money and avoids exposure to harmful chemicals often found in commercially produced cleansers. (Printed: $10.95; eBook: $6.95; Set: $14.95, at www.healthylifepress.com). Available Spring 2012.

The Secret of Singing Springs, by Monte Swan. One Colorado family's treasure-hunting adventure along the trail of Jesse James (Fall 2012).

12838771R00126

Made in the USA
Charleston, SC
01 June 2012